Winning Habits

Winning Habits
Techniques for Excellence in Sports

B. P. Bam

An imprint of Pearson Education

ISBN 978-81-317-1028-9

First Impression, 2008

Published by Dorling Kindersley (India) Pvt. Ltd., licensees of Pearson Education in South Asia.

Head Office: 7th Floor, Knowledge Boulevard, A-8(A), Sector-62, Noida – 201309, U.P, India.
Registered Office: 11 Community Centre, Panchsheel Park, New Delhi 110 017, India.

Typeset by Data Vision, New Delhi.

Digitally Printed in India by Saurabh Printers Pvt. Ltd. in the year of 2013.

To those
who achieve excellence
through grit and persistence
despite overwhelming adversities

Contents

List of Illustrations

Message

It was a pleasure to read this book. I think this book gives a thorough synopsis of an athlete's psychology. It also gives insights into simple and practical techniques, which athletes can use to better their performance in their chosen sport.

I consider myself fortunate to have been under Mr Bam's guidance over the past few years. I have experimented with many of the concepts mentioned in this book, and they have benefited me tremendously. Specifically, they have helped me improve my ability to concentrate for long periods of time and handle the pressure before competition.

The part where he has cited my example reminded me of how lazy and immature I was back then. I am grateful to him for helping me cure that attitude as it was vital to do so.

Overall, I think the book is very well written and therefore provides an easy understanding of the concepts mentioned. It also provides easy solutions to problems that linger in athletes' minds and affect their performances adversely. I would surely recommend this book to every aspiring athlete.

Aparna Popat
Arjuna Award winner
International badminton champion

Foreword
by Rahul Dravid

I first met Mr Bam eight years ago, after learning about his work with some elite sportsmen in the country. In the course of the last eight years, I have had various interactions with him and have learnt a lot about the mind and its control, essential for any serious sportsman. What impresses me about Mr Bam is his simplicity, and clarity of thoughts and ideas gained over the years from experience not only in his work with sportsmen, but also in his job as a successful police officer.

I am glad he has written this book that is full of great knowledge and ideas, which will help all sportsmen who are keen to make a mark at the elite level. His techniques are simple, yet effective in achieving the right frame of mind. One hopes that young people will use this book and learn how to enhance their performance. Many sportsmen have benefited from the ideas discussed in this book. The beauty of these yoga techniques is that they can be used both by the top sportsmen as well as the young athletes just beginning their journey in the world of sports.

I wish Mr Bam and this book all the very best and hope that it will also be translated into various languages. This will benefit the sportsmen immensely, especially since many of them these days come from smaller towns, or even villages, and their exposure to the mental and psychological aspects of sports may be limited.

Foreword
by Geet Sethi

My first interaction with Mr Bam left an indelible impression on my mind. He was, at that time, a deputy commissioner of police in charge of Sahar Airport in Mumbai. His passion for sports 20 years ago was as all-consuming as it is today. His interactions with sportspersons from varied disciplines and his experiments with mental techniques over two decades have made him an authority on sports psychology in India.

The greatness of this book lies in its austere simplicity—much like the man himself. Mr Bam's commitment to sports psychology and his grasp of the subject reveals itself in every chapter of this absorbing book. Anyone who loves sports, irrespective of the standards achieved, will gain immensely from the decades of experience and experiments, which have been documented here.

The idea of giving suggestions, keeping in mind specific sports, towards the concluding part of the book is relevant and will hugely benefit those who want to understand and improve their mental strength.

This is without doubt a must-read for sportspersons and coaches who want to overcome the mental blocks, which prevent them from achieving their potential. Personally, I have benefited greatly with my constant interaction with him. I remember the time in the early 1990s when he recognized the staleness creeping into my system and actually advised me to stop practising. He, then, introduced me to the technique of visualization, which helped me achieve a 1276 world-record break in the 1992 World Professional Billiards Championship.

This is the work of a genius and I would strongly urge all stakeholders of sports to read this book.

Foreword
by Anjali Bhagwat

A very hyper, bubbly, unsteady and overconfident teenager at the shooting range would almost seem like the wrong person at the wrong place, leave alone the possibility of her taking up shooting as a profession. But one person's efforts and vision transformed her into becoming India's leading shooter at the Olympics, the Asian Games and the shooting World Cup tournaments, and eventually reaching the No. 1 ranking in the world. Yes, that's me!

Being in the sport of shooting I realized the true meaning of a mentor, and I am grateful to my guide, B. P. Bam, who is responsible for my transformation into a mature, world-class shooter.

Initially, shooting was physically laborious for us. It involved holding the rifle and just shooting at the target. But realizing our enthusiasm and talent, Mr Bam decided to provide the means and the right environment for our progress. Mr Sanjay Chakravarty took up the responsibility of technical training, while Mr Bam shouldered the task of our mental training.

As we progressed, we improved technically, and simultaneously realized the importance of mental training. I attribute my basic knowledge of yoga to Mr Bam. It began as a compulsion and continued later as a passion; thereafter, it became a responsibility; and now it is a requirement.

Having reached this far, when I look back, I can say that shooting is a game primarily of concentration. To compete at the national level, one requires aggression and a positive attitude. Confidence is another important factor, which is important for success at the international level. Higher-level World Cup tournaments and world-championship performances require focus and patience, while the finals demand sharp reflexes. All these qualities were instilled in me by Mr Bam using the technique of 'circle of excellence', while Pranayama helped me take control of my mind.

During my journey through mental training, I experienced the positive changes in myself. I am a more mature person now who does not get excited or anxious due to petty, insignificant incidents. This attribute helps me particularly during the finals when the mind experiences the adrenaline rush due to nervousness and excitement, and yet the last shot has to be as perfect as possible. Although thoroughly trained, to remember and utilize the right skills at the right moment became possible only due to the strategies of using verbal and non-verbal cues and signals taught by Mr Bam.

While reading this book, I relived the journey of my own sporting career and am extremely happy that this refined, tried and tested knowledge is readily available to any sportsperson who aims at reaching the pinnacle. It gives me immense pride and pleasure to dedicate my achievements and success to my mentor, Mr B. P. Bam.

Developing Indian sports into a formidable force at the international level using available resources has been a cherished dream of his. I wish that all Indian sportspersons utilize the vast knowledge-reserve in this book and fulfil his dreams. This would be the best and most valuable offering to Mr Bam from the world of sports.

Preface

I was very lucky to get introduced to Captain Solomon Jacob Ezekiel, the rifle- and pistol-shooting coach. I learnt a lot about the fascinating sport of target shooting from him, but the real gift I got from him was the concept of mental training. He was so passionate about the idea that he would bring this topic in any discussion within a few minutes. We used to make fun of him for his obsession. But when I actually tried out what he suggested, in target shooting to start with, and in billiards and snooker later, I was simply astonished. I tried to play these sports competitively after I was well past forty, when normally other sportsmen retire, or think of retiring. But I could win quite a few matches, sometimes against better players, and then I realized the value of what Captain, as we used to call the old man, was trying to tell us.

Later, in 1982, when I got bedridden for over four months with severe disc prolapse, commonly known as the slipped disc, my body refusing to cooperate with me was a shock for me. Captain heaped a lot of books on mental training around me and made me read those. He would visit me quite often and we used to have detailed discussions on what I had read. I was surprised to learn that some of the techniques used by the Russians for developing focus and skill were based on the concepts from the Indian science of yoga. I, then, tried to study yoga and also discovered that yoga was developed in ancient India as psychology (did you know that?).

As I studied more about yoga and experimented with yogic techniques, I found that we possessed a great treasure but did not value it. My first experiment involved using visualization for getting well and recovering from my ailment and a miracle took place. Dr A. V. Bavdekar, a renowned orthopaedic surgeon, who was treating me, was of the opinion that the problem I had was so complicated that I would not be able to get well without an operation. The second, third and fourth opinions also had confirmed his diagnosis. But I argued with myself that the techniques of visualization were being used by the Olympic and world champions in conditioning their physique and responses. I thought that getting well from any illness also meant conditioning one's body, and these techniques should serve that purpose also.

I set up my own schedules of visualization. Prior to the visualization sessions, I practised Nyasa, a technique for relaxation developed by a sect of yogis. Then I used to visualize the tests the doctor used to conduct for checking my progress; some of these were leg-raising, bending and twisting. I imagined that the pain was bearable and the doctor was telling me that the operation was no longer required since there was considerable improvement in the condition. It actually materialized and I got well without an operation. Dr Bavdekar often used to say that it was a miracle that he would have found hard to believe had he not seen it himself. Subsequently, I witnessed several such miracles not only in my own experiences, but in the case of others also.

Playing billiards and snooker league matches and handicap tournaments gave me a chance to get introduced to a number of legendary greats like Wilson Jones, Michael Ferreira, Om Agarwal, Geet Sethi and several other top performers. I used to play for Om Agarwal's team and he would wonder how my performance in the match would always be better than that in the practice session. He, then, started experimenting with the techniques and went on to win the world amateur snooker title. Subsequently, Geet Sethi, Devendra Joshi, Subhash Agarwal, Ashok Shandilya and a number of other players picked up the techniques and used them successfully.

In target shooting, Ashok Pandit, Sheila Kanungo, Anjali Bhagwat, Suma Shirur and Deepali used to practise at the Worli Shooting Complex in Mumbai, which was frequented by me even after the sad demise of Captain Ezekiel. We, then, set up a weekly clinic for sports psychology, which was also attended by other top sportsmen. The great badminton star

Prakash Padukone established his academy in Bangalore and requested me to hold workshops for the trainees regularly. There, I had the luck of meeting P. Gopichand, Aparna Popat, Deepankar Bhattacharya, Manjusha Kanwar and many other top badminton players.

Jatin Paranjape was the first cricketer of renown who came to me for counselling. Thereafter, other cricketers also came for the same purpose. I felt thrilled to get phone calls for appointment from all famous sportsmen like Rahul Dravid and Sachin Tendulkar. Discussions with these people taught me a lot about the game of cricket, which I had not played beyond the school level, and I started enjoying it as a spectator more than before. I organized workshops for the Ranji Trophy teams of Mumbai and Karnataka, and also for the cricket umpires of the BCCI.

Harmeet Kahlon was the first golfer to come to me for consultation. I, subsequently, organized some workshops for the Indian Golf Union and met Donato Di Ponziano, the renowned Italian coach in golf. I wrote a few articles in the golf magazine, *Golfingly Yours*, published from Delhi. It was such a pleasure working with golfers and watching them play. I felt very sad that I was never able to play this wonderful game. I experienced the same feeling when I worked with the mountaineering team of Maharashtra going on the Everest expedition. After all, how many games can a person play in the limited span of one life?

Some of the renowned players I worked with in the earlier days were of the opinion that only those who had performed at a high level would understand the concepts of sports psychology properly. But when I worked in the experiment of Kreeda Prabodhini* carried out by the Government of Maharashtra, I found that it is better to introduce these concepts to serious sportsmen at the beginning of their careers. Then, it becomes easy for them to meet the challenges

---

* Kreeda Prabodhini is a government-run sports academy in Nashik, which was founded in 1996 and specializes in pistol- and rifle-shooting training programmes.

of competitive sports with confidence. In Kreeda Prabodhini, I worked with schoolboys who had just taken up the game of target shooting. I had to speak to them in Marathi to explain the concepts to them. Their coaches, who had worked with me earlier, understood the concepts better and also improved their performances in national championships. The boys too picked up the game very fast and achieved success in good measure. At whatever level you play, these concepts help you perform better and give you a lot of satisfaction.

Amongst the Western authors, Terry Orlick, Charles Garfield, Shane Murphy, James E. Loehr, Bob Rotella and Stephen Covey have been my favourites. As regards the science of yoga, I based my study on the Bhagavad Gita, Upanishads and the Patanjali Yoga Darshan. My favourite commentators have been Acharya Vinoba Bhave, P. Y. Deshpande and Acharya K. K. Kolhatkar. I was extremely lucky to have A. L. Bhagwat as my spiritual guru. He was a practising yogi and a follower of the sect known as Nath Pantha. Later on, I had another stroke of luck in getting to know Pandurang Shastri Athavale, the originator of the worldwide movement of Swadhyay.* I used to approach either of them whenever any concept or thought was not clear to me. (This would happen quite often.) Both these great scholars were very tolerant towards me and they had a knack of explaining the most difficult concepts in simple terms with the help of day-to-day examples.

My approach had been to go to the books only when I had problems, study only the concerned part, and be happy with the solutions found, and their practical applications. I have not studied the Gita, Upanishads and Yoga Darshan in depth, which I intend to do now, if time permits. But I am convinced that these scriptures have plenty to offer for our ordinary challenges also. Somehow, there is a common belief that only those who are interested in attaining moksha, or deliverance, should read these. It is true that they can be of

---

* Swadhyay Parivar is an organization spread all over the world and does a lot of humanitarian, cultural and spiritual work.

great help for achieving that goal. But it is also true for the goals in any other field. Can this science, which helps you to reach the top of the Everest, not help you scale the small hillock near your residence? Believe me, our practical problems are seldom more serious than that.

Till I retired from the police service, it was very difficult for me to take out time for this hobby, which included studying yoga and Western psychology, and experimenting with the practical application of the techniques. Yet, I kept on studying and experimenting whenever possible. There was no time for systematic documentation of the experiments. After retirement, I could get together a good team to work for the Purushottam Academy, which I founded in 1996 for the promotion of excellence in all fields. The planning and writing of this book would not have been possible without the assistance of Madhuli Khodke, a practising psychologist; Sandeep Jadhav, who is a devoted student of the science of yoga; and Prashant Kulkarni, a colleague from Swadhyay. My wife Sudha has also been of great help, first, by bearing with me for according top priority to these hobbies, and then by being the first critical reader of everything I wrote.

I shall be very happy if dedicated sportspersons find the techniques given in this book useful. I am sure if yogic scholars, along with sports enthusiasts, undertake a serious research, many more practical techniques can be found. Achievers in every field will benefit immensely from that effort. Till then, this is all I have to offer.

B. P. Bam

PART I

BASIC CONCEPTS

1

Be a Warrior

In the 1940s, Mr Ghouse Mohammed was the national tennis champion of India for several years and he became the first Indian to reach the quarter-finals in Wimbledon in 1939. We had the luck to have him as the sports director during my college days. A chat with him was always inspiring for all the sportsmen of our college. He was once narrating his experience in his first international exposure. One of the journalists asked him, 'You're going to meet one of the top seeds tomorrow. You do not know his game. How are you going to face him?' Mr Ghouse replied, 'Yes, I do not know his game. But he also does not know my game. We both are playing tennis, which I know how to play. I shall fight and do my best to win.' He caused a major upset in the tournament the next day.

A person participating in competitive sports has to be a warrior to emerge victorious. There is a deep-seated urge in the minds of all human beings to excel and to prove one's superiority over others. This urge has led to most of the fights, battles and wars in human history resulting in bloodshed and destruction. Rewards for victory would be different depending on the conditions, but losers were invariably punished with death. Those who did not fight themselves, loved to hear the stories of valour.

Later on, fights amongst gladiators became very popular in ancient Rome. The spectators used to derive vicarious pleasure identifying themselves with the winners. But the punishment for losing was still death. As civilization advanced, the concept of competitive sports evolved as the remedy to satisfy this urge to excel without the violence involved in fights and battles. But the attitude of spectators remains the same.

Be a Warrior

Once international competitions started, winning in sports events became a matter of national pride. That trend still continues and all nations take pride in their players emerging at the top in such competitions. The Olympic Movement and the other international games being held at regular intervals became popular, but the basic instincts were the same. Everyone concerned wanted to establish the superiority of his nation by winning maximum number of medals in international competitions. This was a very welcome development, for sports became a substitute for war. After the Second World War, one of the European thinkers had commented that the Olympic Movement must be sustained and developed, since the only alternative available to it was war.

An Award Ceremony

In neighbouring countries, which entertain inimical feelings against each other, sports serve as a substitute for war. After the Kargil War (1998) between India and Pakistan, there was a serious debate whether the cricket teams of India and Pakistan should play against each other. Matches between the teams of these two countries are usually fought out as fiercely as real battles. People in both the countries await the results with the same curiosity and anxiety. One of the top sportsmen in India was asked whether the cricket tours between India and Pakistan should resume on the background of Kargil. He made a cryptic remark, 'There should be cricket series and no Kargils!'

Because of the origin of combats and battles, winning is normally linked with killer instinct. It is misunderstood as being ruthless in killing and sometimes as blind rage. Even for a warrior fighting an actual battle involving matter of life and death, a clear perception of the situation, alert focus, split-second decisions and their accurate execution are the essential ingredients required to win. For achieving all these, he has to have a superb control over all his thoughts, emotions and inner faculties. Unless he can exercise this control, the chances of his winning are very remote. The situation in which Lord Krishna narrated the Bhagavad Gita to Arjuna illustrates this point very well.

This conversation takes place at the beginning of the war at Kurukshetra. Both the armies are poised to strike at each other. At that time, in between the two armies, the two best warriors on the Pandava side are discussing yoga and the methods of controlling the mind, intellect, and other inner faculties. Some people erroneously think that this discussion was irrelevant to the situation. But this inference is totally wrong. Falling prey to wrong thoughts and emotions, Arjuna had lost the power to wield his bow. He could not even stand up to fight. On top of it, he was trying to justify his inaction by quoting wrong philosophy. Only after a positive counterargument he could be convinced to fight with a serious resolve to win, which he eventually did. A major contribution to the victory of the Pandavas was from Arjuna, who was initially deprived of the will and skill to fight, because of entertaining wrong thoughts and emotions.

Krishna Narrating the Bhagavad Gita to Arjuna

Nowadays, a competitive sportsman has to face similar situations throughout his career. *In any match, the better player does not win; the player who plays better wins.* The same principle applies to team games also. This is proved in almost every tournament time and again. We see seeded players falling on the wayside losing to lesser ranked opponents even in the initial rounds. A corollary of this principle is that if you have won the previous match against a particular opponent, it does not mean that you will win again this time. Similarly, if you have lost to a previous opponent in a previous meeting, you *need not* write yourself off in this match also.

The basic responsibility is to prove your calibre by performing better than the opponent in every match or competition. Then, alone, you have the chance of becoming a champion.

Though most of the sports involve non-verbal skills (chess being a glorious exception) manifesting through physical actions, the inner faculties, commonly referred to as the mind, play a major role. According to the science of yoga, all physical activities originate in the mind which takes all the decisions, while the body merely executes them.

In competitive sports, split-second decisions and correct responses to signals are essential factors. A large number of responses are stored in the memory. Identifying the signals correctly and producing the accurate response, including some improvization if need be, is the real challenge. Human mind has the power of leaving the time and space frame and wandering about in the past or the future and anywhere else at will. It likes to form habits so that the responses emerge from memory automatically and it remains free to roam about. These habits form your comfort zone and limit your performance.

Repeated physical practice is supposed to form the correct habits so that proper response is ensured every time. If this was easy, every practice session would have brought about improvement in performance. But the mind does not like to form new habits and keeps on producing wrong responses from memory. So many players keep suffering in this regard! In practice sessions they perform brilliantly but in matches they fail to produce the same brilliance. This happens simply because the mind refuses to leave the old habit of producing wrong responses.

Habits of entertaining negative or irrelevant thoughts, allowing the controls to be hijacked by wrong emotions, cutting off the flow of energy and skill by allowing wrong responses have ruined the careers of many talented and promising players. They are unable to break away from the wrong habits and to replace them by correct ones and soon, either give up, or continue to perform miserably losing to ordinary players. There was a famous quote by a British sports writer, 'Our [cricket] team has become such an expert in losing that it will manage to lose the match even if there are no opponents in the field.'

Some of the common complaints of such players are:

- I am a late starter. In the initial stages I cannot perform to my capacity.
- I can win only if the opponent is leading.
- I find it very difficult to win the last point and have lost matches even when serving for match point.
- I cannot reproduce my practice form in matches or competitions.
- I cannot play well with a better opponent; or worse still, I cannot focus when I am playing a lower ranked player.
- I cannot beat this particular player.
- I cannot perform on a strange court or ground or before spectators.
- When leading in a match, a mistake or a wrong decision irritates me so much that I lose some more negative points.
- I hate waiting for the match to start.
- I cannot perform well unless the conditions are ideal.

The list can be never-ending. On the face of it, they appear very foolish and one wonders why the players should allow themselves to be tortured by such negative thoughts, knowing fully well that these will ruin their careers, putting to waste all their time and efforts towards improvement.

The remedy for this lies in breaking those bad habits which lead one to poor performance, and cultivating those habits which can lead one to victory. Lots of efforts in the proper direction are needed. Let us examine those in the subsequent chapters.

ACTION POINTS

- A person participating in competitive sports has to be a warrior to emerge victorious.
- Always think positive and do not lose your focus.
- The better player does not win; the player who plays better wins.
- The basic responsibility is to prove your calibre by performing better than the opponent in every match or competition.
- According to the science of yoga, all physical activity originates in the mind, which takes all the decisions while the body merely executes them.
- Identifying the signals correctly and producing the accurate response, including some improvization, if need be, is the real challenge.
- Cultivating proper habits can lead you to victory.

2

Worship of Excellence

Meditate at Dawn

The science of yoga has classified the inner faculties into four categories according to the functions they perform. There is consciousness or *chitta*, which experiences the world through the senses and builds up memory. Then there is ego, which is the core of your personality and functions through likes and dislikes. The intellect tries to perceive objects and events in their true form and stores the knowledge. The mind looks into the future and tries to anticipate whether the course of events will be good or bad. In common parlance all these four are normally referred to as the mind. There is one more power which is a special gift to all human beings. It is the power of communication known as *wani* or speech. The mind including the other three faculties experiences the world, and the *wani* verbalizes the experiences. That is how we learn anything, either by experiencing it ourselves, or learning about the experiences of others by means of words.

There is one more power, the subconscious or the inner power, which is closest to the indwelling God or the *atman*, and it supervises the functioning of the inner faculties and the power of communication. The mind has the capacity of remaining focused, and also the capacity of defocusing and to keep shifting the focus every moment. When it is focused, all the inner faculties are concentrating only on a selected object or event and the verbal thoughts, if any, are brought forth by the *wani*. Both the powers of focus and defocus are essential for day-to-day life. In focus the inner power is controlling the inner faculties. But they do not like to be controlled in this fashion. They form habits, which govern our thoughts, emotions, and responses. Once habits are formed, the inner faculties do not have to pay much attention to what is happening and they can roam about freely.

Now some habits may be useful to achieve our goals. If you are lucky, you may have more such habits. But mostly, habits lead you astray and away from the path of your goal. The practical side of yoga deals with identifying the unwanted habits, dropping them, and cultivating the habits which will keep you on the correct path. By not exercising the choice of focus and remaining defocused, you become the slave of your habits and lose control over the line of thinking, feelings and responses. You get so used to this way of life that you completely forget the fact that you have the choice of focus. Unless you exercise it by disciplining the inner faculties, life becomes like a boat being carried away by wind and waves, without any control. The result is failure and misery. Yoga teaches us the methods to discipline these faculties and take over command. Otherwise, we live like an inefficient ruler, whose generals and ministers have usurped the command and stopped listening to him. Finally, they put him in jail and take over the reigns. But they do not have the capacity to rule, and again, the result is misery.

The first thing to do is to find out the real reason for your doing anything. Ask yourself why you are doing it and the answer will give you the reasons for the choice. There may be a deep-seated urge or liking to choose a particular field or sport. If this urge is identified and strengthened, it helps building up a commitment to the path leading towards the goal. If you love what you are doing, it can be done very well and the chances of success improve. But you can choose only the field and not the challenges in it. These are thrown at you and they have to be faced as they come. Sometimes, you do not have the choice of selecting even the field. If you keep resenting and getting annoyed, you are sure to lose form, and success will elude you.

Just as you can do a thing of your choice and like it very well, accepting a challenge is another feeling which can lead you to your goals. Every player likes to play his game, but the hardships required to get the wherewithal and to cultivate the skills required are mostly hated.

It was 1996, when Aparna Popat, India's star badminton player was a junior. I was watching her perform the physical fitness schedules at Prakash Padukone Academy in Bangalore. While jogging and later doing the shadow training, her face appeared contorted as if she was enduring some pain. I stopped her and asked whether something was wrong and if she was having some problem. At that time she said she was all right, but later during the individual session, she admitted that she hated the physical fitness exercises and loved only to play badminton. Luckily, she is a very intelligent person and I could convince her that by hating what she was doing, she would build up only an adversarial attitude to the training and would not benefit from it at all. Such an attitude, once developed, gets carried over into the actual game. In that case, Aparna could have lost interest in the game itself. Then any improvement would have been impossible and even maintaining the same level would have been difficult. I suggested that she should take up the fitness schedules as a challenge. She loves to face a challenge and felt convinced. Later on, I found that she had become very particular about the fitness schedules. Very soon she won the senior national title and at the time of writing this, she is still holding on to it even after several years.

Reinforcing the commitment by identifying the inner urge or drive and also the challenges has to be a continuous process throughout the career of a sportsperson. Unless this is ensured, the willingness to face hardships will disappear. The will to sacrifice and stay away from distractions also gets weakened. Then the discipline required for building up the stamina, strength and skill will also vanish, destroying all the chances of winning.

Two habits which are interlinked have to be avoided at all costs. The memory keeps playing tricks and you remember only what you want to forget. The past mistakes and failures are remembered so often that they get etched into the memory. They then creep into the system and the same mistakes keep occurring repeatedly with alarming frequency. This leads to the second habit of getting afraid of the future. Fretting over past mistakes and worrying about future are two of the worst habits that can lead us to misery.

How do you get rid of these two wrong habits? Keeping the focus on excellence and honouring it whenever it manifests itself is the key. Once this habit is formed you are never afraid of your opponent's excellence, for it works as a cue for your best to come out. That is when it is needed most. You can be a champion only if you can produce a better skill and form than the opponent when he is playing at his best. Hoping that the opponent will play badly in order that you may win, will spell disaster for your plans.

Anjali Bhagwat, Suma Shirur and Deepali Deshpande make a formidable trio in the field of rifle shooting. All the three were brilliant students and were looking for jobs after completing graduation, where they had secured first class marks. They could have chosen careers in All India Civil Services, which I had even suggested to them, but they opted for lower level jobs which would give them sufficient time to practise rifle shooting. They had the dream of winning gold medals in international competitions and hear the Indian national anthem being played during the medal ceremonies. Resolutely facing adverse conditions throughout their careers they have realized this dream several times over. Their sacrifice and dedication have brought prominence to India in international target shooting and have inspired several young men and women to take up the sport. Financial problems pestered them quite a bit. But the worship of excellence has taken them to the top in their sport and they have won cash rewards worth millions of rupees. They are now able to pursue their interests in comparative comfort.

There is a lot of talk about spotting and promoting talent. But experience shows that mere talent can help only in a few early successes. Once the player moves to the higher categories, failures start occurring and it is very difficult to cope up with them. Talent has to be backed up by total commitment and dedication to the goals for cultivating the skills required for emerging victorious. Lacking these qualities, a large number of talented persons have underperformed. As against that, there are many who had very little talent, but they have managed to reach the top and remain there for considerable period just by total commitment to excellence. Talent is a gift of God, but you need not worry if you do not possess it. Commitment and dedication will carry you to the goal with greater certainty. No skill or achievement is beyond you if you make the resolve.

Whenever you think of future, the problem of a steady livelihood looms large. Normally everyone wants an assured, cozy future, and that too, at the earliest. This is where dedication and resolve come into play. Yoga tells us that if you worship excellence, keep your focus on it, it gets transmitted into you and then you just do not have to worry about the livelihood at all, for, prosperity is bound to follow true excellence.

There are no substitutes for commitment, dedication and hard work. Make these your habits and you will become not only invincible, but also prosperous.

ACTION POINTS

- The mind has the capacity of remaining focused and also the capacity of defocusing and shifting the focus every moment.

- The inner faculties form habits, which govern your thoughts, emotions and responses.

- The practical side of yoga deals with identifying the unwanted habits and cultivating the habits which will keep you on the right path.

- Just as you can do a thing of your choice and like it very well, accepting a challenge is another feeling which can lead you to your goals.

- Fretting over past mistakes and worrying about the future are two of the worst habits that can lead you to misery.

- You can be a champion only if you can produce a better skill and form than the opponent, even when he is playing at his best.

- According to yoga, if you worship excellence and keep your focus on it, it gets transmitted into you. Then you need not worry about the livelihood at all, for prosperity is bound to follow true excellence.

3

Goal-setting and Planning

Once you get committed to the sport you have chosen, you should set your goals and also identify the challenges you have to face. Every goal should be realistic and spelt out in clear terms. The stages through which you can achieve your goal should be worked out and described in lucid terms. Your analyses about your present capabilities and how you can develop further the ability required should also be very clear. Just having a vague goal and not planning the efforts properly will lead you nowhere. Writing down the goals will give you a good idea about the efforts required and their direction.

The long-term goals should be finalized first, before you get down to fixing the short-term goals and the various stages that have to be achieved. Becoming the world champion or winning the Olympic Gold can be a very attractive goal, but to achieve it you will have to start winning the local competitions and then come to the state- and national-level events. You will have to qualify yourself for participating in world championships or the Olympics.

Fixing the time frame for each of these phases is very important. Actually time is the only commodity which is in limited supply. You must achieve all the goals within the time available to you. You can get all the equipment, financial support and guidance needed, but you cannot add even a single hour to the time available. Once you start your planning, you realize how short the time at your disposal is. Break up the journey to your goals into intervals and plan every interval carefully. A week is a very good unit of time to plan your preparation and improvement, but make it a habit to try and execute your schedules with total dedication.

Just as you should not spare your opponent once the competition starts, you should not spare yourself during the practice sessions and also during the match. That does not mean you should overstrain during preparation or overexert during the match. It is careful planning which will enable you to take the overload required for increasing your fitness and improving the skill level required for winning the match.

Mere practice is never enough and you have to obtain the valuable experience of playing matches. Handling match pressures is a skill which can be learned only during matches. Your planning should therefore include practice matches and even some of the tournaments should be played with the goal of obtaining match practice. These days, various tournaments are being held in almost all sports throughout the year. You should not try to play and win every tournament and exhaust yourself before the major event. Matches and tournaments are won not on the regular stamina and strength. The effort to remain focused itself consumes huge amount of energy. Fatigue is a big problem in the effort to win. If you are fatigued you become unsure about your strength and abilities. Then you become tentative in your decisions and unnecessarily defensive in your approach. To become a champion you need the courage to take quick, precise decisions.

In planning the training overload, the idea is not only to build up the skill but also the strength, stamina and the energy reserves. During the competition season, these reserves are to be used up and have to be replenished later. No match is won on the regular strength and stamina. You have to draw on the reserves. When the competitions were few and far between, the athletes could train harder during the off seasons and develop the reserves. But currently there are so many competitions being organized round the year. Almost in every sport the professional players have to keep on travelling and playing various tournaments. They expend the energy much faster and the need to create reserves is felt by them very acutely. If this is not done, injuries and illness force themselves on the player, compelling him/her to take rest and replenish the lost energy.

Earlier, it was believed that the peak form and the top fitness level of a sportsman should coincide with the most important competition of the season. Nowadays, however, players do not get enough time gap between two major tournaments. The human body is a part of nature and functions in a particular rhythm of exertion and rest. When you are planning the building up of strength, stamina and skills along with energy reserves, you should take into consideration this biological rhythm. The top competitions where you can perform at peak should be selected in consultation with the coach. Then the training between the gaps should be properly planned keeping in mind the requirement of breaks for rest and diversions. In the time available, there should be a period for gradual increase in the training overload and then the player should check the excess overload and remain in a maintenance phase during the period of actual competitions.

Dr Morehouse, one of the leading sports psychologists from the USA, recommends that before planning the training overload, the player should ask himself/herself the question: 'fit for what?' The fitness exercises chosen should be conducive to the skill required for the sport. By regular practice of the skill, the energy acquired during the training has to be converted into the one required for that particular skill. Along with the strength and stamina, the body also needs suppleness and muscular coordination for executing the skills, and special attention has to be paid to the trunk region and the joints. Yogasanas are useful for this purpose and should be executed during both the energy reserve building and the maintenance phases.

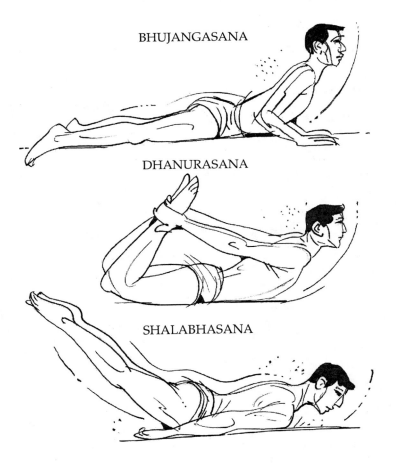

BHUJANGASANA

DHANURASANA

SHALABHASANA

Yogasanas

The muscles containing most of the energy reserves are located around the spine. There are special exercise schedules available to develop these muscles besides some specific yogasanas like Bhujangasana, Shalabhasana, Dhanurasana, Pashimatanasana, Ardha Matsyendrasana, etc. In consultation with the fitness experts, these should be included in the training programmes. Sufficient provision should be made for rest, relaxation and diversions; otherwise the mind becomes stale and bored. Then it is very difficult to maintain the performance level.

Geet Sethi, the seven times world champion in billiards, had once come to me with the problem of boredom and loss of interest in the game. He had lost in the first round of a major competition and was expected to defend his title in the world championships, which were just a couple of months away. The staleness and boredom had killed his will and the skill to win. I then suggested that he should stay away from billiards for at least a month and should not even touch the cue during that period. He was shocked with the idea itself. For traditional thought had prescribed maximum amount of practice during the period available. I could convince him that such a withdrawal from the game would re-awaken his love for the game, improve his focus and he would start winning again. He had made provision for several hours of practice during that period and was wondering what he should do with that time. I suggested that he spent it playing some other sport to his liking and give more time to his family, which would make all of them happy reflecting that mood in his match preparation also.

Geet agreed to do this and I was really impressed by the commitment of this great player, when after three weeks, he asked me whether he should start practising again. He felt the eagerness of a fresh lover and wanted to prepare for a tournament being held after a week. I convinced him that he did not need any practice for that tournament and should try to increase his deep-seated drive to play the game he loved. He risked going through the experiment and won that tournament comfortably. Regular practice for just the remaining month could get his old form back and he went on to win the world title with his usual poise.

Both long-term and short-term goals should be very realistic. If you set up an impossible goal before you, your own mind and intellect will have doubts about your ability to do so. And doubts can be very destructive. At the same time, you should not underestimate your capacities. The correct way is to analyse your present form and level properly and place the goal just one step ahead.

Deepankar Bhattacharya has been a very talented and renowned badminton player. He has won the national singles title thrice consecutively, in the years 1993, 1994, 1995. In 1998, he had been beset with injuries and illness. He was doubtful about his form and was wondering what goal he should set up before himself for the national championships which were round the corner. We sat and analysed his impression about his capacity. He felt that he would be able to reach the quarterfinals. I then suggested that he should set a goal just to win the quarterfinals and visualize himself playing the semifinals. He agreed to do this and easily reached the semifinals, in which he lost to the ultimate winner, Gopichand after a memorable battle.

But it was Suma Shirur, the world champion rifle shooter who gave me a pleasant surprise while proving this point. She was going for the Asian shooting championships and it was her last chance to qualify for the Athens Olympics. She was not in proper form that year and had still managed to reach the score of 399/400 in a major competition. That performance was just one point short of the world record of the perfect score of 400/400. She came to me with the worry that she may not be able to win the Olympic quota place. She was very keen to qualify and participate in the Olympics. During the discussions with her, we recounted together all her previous performances. I reminded her that, even though out of form, her best performance was just one point away from the perfect score. I thought that a shooter of her calibre should not be happy with simply qualifying for the Olympics and told her that she should go for the gold in the Asian championships and make a serious bid for the world record. She agreed that she should make an effort to go to the Olympics as one of the top seeds and not just as a qualifier.

It was a great joy to receive her phone call from Kuala Lumpur, Malaysia, where the championships were held. She had won the gold medal with the perfect score and the world record. In her case also the goal was quite realistic for she was just one step away from it. Being a champion fighter, it was no wonder she could realize her dream. She even reached the finals in the 2004 Athens Olympics, justifying her being amongst the top seeds.

ACTION POINTS

- You should write down the goals and the stages, so that you get a good idea about the efforts required.

- Your planning should include playing in practice matches. Some of the tournaments should be played with the goal of obtaining practice that is valuable for any match.

- The human body is a part of nature and functions in a particular rhythm of exertion and rest.

- If the training overload is planned properly, the system gets a proper message to create sufficient energy reserves.

- Your plans should make provision for rest and diversions. Then the mind will remain fresh to meet challenges.

- The correct way is to analyse your present form and level properly and place the goal just one step ahead.

- A champion is the one who can take quick and proper decisions and has the courage to execute them.

4

Self-image and Confidence

A young snooker player, who had impressed everyone by his talent and had caused major upsets in some of the important tournaments, suddenly disappeared from the scene. When I met him in a function after a long gap, I enquired why he was not playing tournaments. He said he was participating but was totally out of form and was seriously considering giving up playing at least for about six months. He requested for a counselling session to decide how he should train during that period. During the discussions, I asked him what the analyses and suggestions of his coach were. He replied that the coach had suggested putting in more hours of practice and he was practising daily for seven to eight hours. In practice, he was getting his touch back but in matches, his game just did not flourish and he was losing to very ordinary players. I realized that his problem was that of an inadequate self-image and instead of attending to it, he was trying to improve the skill level. I remembered a song my mother used to sing. It was a song criticizing the functioning of civic authorities. 'Fire has broken out in the north of the city and the fire brigade is rushing to the south.' Just a few tips about improving the self-image worked wonders. Instead of giving up the game for six months, he entered a major tournament just a month later and won the final match with a good cash prize. He was badly in need of the money, as well as, the confidence of performing well at a high level. There was a half-page article on his superb touch, which he had totally lost till just about a month back. The magic was done by an improved self-image.

Self-image is your impression about your own capacities and it is the ultimate limit of your achievement. You can never surpass it. If you allow it to remain underdeveloped, no amount of practice to perfect your skill level will help you win. Inadequate self-image indicates that you are not able to express your existing skills properly; then, what is the use of trying to improve the skills?

The concept of self-image can be explained very well by means of an illustration. Suppose you purchase a long

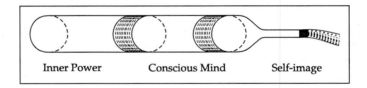

Inner Power   Conscious Mind   Self-image

Figure 4.1

pipe consisting of three pieces to water your garden. Now the first piece of the pipe is the subconscious inner power, which stores all your strength, stamina and the skills required and makes them available in response to signals, whenever needed. The second piece is your conscious mind, which decides the goals and the efforts to be put in to reach those. The third is your self-image, which is actually the delivery pipe. Now the flow of water will depend on the capacity of the piece with the smallest diameter (see Figure 4.1).

Inner Power   Conscious Mind   Self-image

Figure 4.2

A problem should be analysed correctly and the area in which it is occurring has to be identified. If the first piece of the pipe is smaller, it means that the level of the skills acquired is inadequate or the player is lacking in strength or stamina. Then the practice should be directed to development in these areas. If the second piece is of smaller diameter, it means that the efforts being put in to improve the skill are inadequate and the direction itself might be wrong. Then steps have to be taken to put in more quality practice and correct the techniques by getting proper training. But if the third piece is of small diameter, the self-image has to be analysed and improved. It has to be brought to the level of capacities acquired. This is just a question of building up faith in your capacities. If all the three pipes are of the same diameter, the water flow or the skill flow will be the optimum and as a result the performance will be the best. This condition is known as the triad state and is supposed to be the ideal (see Figure 4.2).

Players spend a lot of time practising their skills. But no effort is made to strengthen the faith that the level of skill has improved and they can perform at higher levels. How do you do this? The habit of focusing on mistakes, failures and negative experiences has to be changed. Like the player, most of the parents and coaches also keep the mistakes in constant focus, by mentioning and discussing them frequently. They do not realize that this results in damaging the self-image and leads to further failures. Then there is the public opinion, even that of your so-called well wishers, which keeps reminding you with irritating frequency about where you had gone wrong.

A badminton player had come to me for consultation. She had performed very well in the past but for over a year had not won a single round. She maintained a diary, which she had brought along. In that diary, she had described all her mistakes and failures in minute details. She did this at the instance of her coach, who hoped that the mistakes, once identified, could be removed later. While we were discussing the diary, Anjali Bhagwat and her rifle-shooting colleagues walked in. They also were surprised to see the entries in the diary. Anjali remarked, 'What a perfect way to negativize!' It was no wonder that the player was not able to win a single match. I asked her to stop writing that diary and to shift the focus on thoughts about what she had done well in her previous matches and practice sessions. A few tips about focus brought back her earlier form and she started winning during the same season. She went on to win the state championship and later on her consistency in performance won her the coveted Shiv Chhatrapati Award for consistent high performance in sports.

Another bad habit which damages one's self-image is the urge to justify failures. Everyone is worried about what others think and goes on trying to find excuses for justifying the mistakes. Every attempt to justify failure keeps one's focus only on mistakes and they creep into one's system by repeated visualization. More discussion about this will appear in the chapters on self-talk and visualization. There is a basic rule to remember. *Success does not require justification and failure has none.* However well you try to justify the failures, people are not going to believe that you are a good player. Your performance in competitions is going to stick to you till you make efforts and improve it in subsequent tournaments. Only winning the subsequent matches will convince others of the level of your performance. Then why take all the trouble to keep on justifying verbally and in the process damaging your self-image?

One of the top badminton players from India had created quite a flutter by causing a couple of upsets by beating higher ranked players in the 1990 Commonwealth Games. She suddenly found herself in the semifinals. Her self-image was not equal to this challenge. Consequently, her performance in the semifinals and the match to decide the third and fourth places was so poor that everyone started wondering how she reached that level.

In the same Commonwealth Games, Ashok Pandit was participating in the centre fire pistol event. Since he was in good form, we were expecting a medal from him. A press conference was arranged before his departure. He told the journalists that he was going to win the gold medal and also make a bid for the Games record. He told them to keep their copies ready, promising to convey from the venue whether he had broken the record or not. One of the journalists asked me whether this should be published, because no Indian shooter had won a gold medal in the Commonwealth Games till then, leave alone making records. He was thinking that Ashok would come under pressure if this were published in advance. I had a very good idea about Ashok's self-image and fighting spirit. He had the capacity to perform better under pressure. I asked the pressmen to go ahead and publish the interview verbatim, which they did. Ashok went on to win the gold medal with a new record, which remained unbroken for several years.

Self-image depends on the faith in your own self; on what you focus from your past and how you expect to meet the challenges in future. It forms a comfort zone for performance. If you are performing below your comfort zone, you produce a sudden brilliance and reach the level accepted by you in your self-image. If you start performing at a level higher than your expectations, you start wondering how this is happening and start making mistakes pulling the performance down to the level of expectation.

'Focus on your excellence' is the key to building a proper self-image. Do not take your brilliance for granted. Keep a sharp look-out for it to start appearing. Reinforce it in your memory by verbalizing and visualizing it again and again. Then you get the courage to see yourself facing challenges well in future. Visualizing your self handling the challenges in a future event with confidence is also of great help for building up self-image. Controlling both verbal and non-verbal thoughts through self-talk and visualization are of tremendous help in building up and maintaining proper self-image. We will see about that in the subsequent chapters.

ACTION POINTS

- For winning, drop the habit of keeping focus on mistakes and failures. Shift the focus to positive experiences.

- The habit of focusing on mistakes, failures and negative experiences has to be changed.

- Every attempt to justify failure keeps the focus on mistakes and they creep into your system by repeated visualization.

- Success does not require justification and failure has none.

- Self-image depends on the faith you have in your own self.

- 'Focus on excellence' is the key to building up a proper self-image.

5

Self-talk: Controlling Verbal Thoughts

One of the top pistol shooters had a bad habit of describing his mistakes and failures in great details. Whenever asked about a match, he would go on talking about his bad shots at length. Obviously the purpose was to justify the below-par performance. I realized that talking to him affected my own performance adversely. These mistakes started creeping into my system also, besides being clearly etched in his muscle memory. I tried to convince him that this negativization of thoughts was spoiling his performance, but he would not give up. Finally, I had to issue instructions to the shooters training with me, not to talk to him, at least before their matches. I am quite sure that this shooter did not reach anywhere near his potential and the habit of dwelling on the bad shots contributed a lot to his underperformance.

All actions originate in the mind, and *wani* or the power of communication plays a role by introducing verbal thoughts. The mind experiences the world through the senses and *wani* adds to this knowledge by learning about the experience of others through words. It also helps in drawing inferences about events, which you have not experienced directly. Both good and bad experiences are stored in your memory and verbal thoughts awaken these experiences when you are playing. To optimize your performance, you will have to train yourself to control your verbal thoughts and the responses to them.

In all our thought processes, words matter a lot, especially those words in which we have faith. When they come from a knowledgeable person, or one who is describing his own experience, faith is established quite naturally. If the words are describing your own experience, you tend to believe them totally. If you go on listening to a description of mistakes or you yourself keep describing your negative actions, the inner power gets a wrong message that you want these responses to be repeated. Then you go on getting surprised at your poor show.

Another power of words is that they build up faith in you if you go on listening to them or uttering them repeatedly. Most of the publicity and propaganda drives exploit this fact to the maximum. By frequent recommendation of a brand by your heroes or role models, you tend to believe that the product is really the best and find yourself buying it. Dr Goebels, Hitler's propaganda expert, believed and proved that if a lie is repeated hundred times, people start believing it to be the truth. As far as possible, avoid listening to such misleading words, but if they are coming from your bosses, spouses, coaches or even fans, I do not know any sure method to avoid listening to them. The only way available is to build up your defences strongly by a well-developed self-talk. Then you can protect your self-image and ability to perform.

Om Agarwal, India's first world champion in snooker, played a match against an upcoming player. Om was not in good form and lost the first frame badly. His wily opponent passed a remark to a spectator, making sure that Om would hear it, 'Om is finished now. He is not the same player whom everybody feared.' Om lost his temper and also the match playing a worse game. When I asked him what happened, he flew into rage again and described how he got angry about the remark and could not play properly. I was surprised at this unprofessional attitude. If the opponents know that you can be thrown off gear by a nasty remark, anyone can beat you. I said, 'He only uttered these words; you went on to prove him right. Actually, his remark should have made you focus more and produce your best form. If you could have beaten him and proved him wrong, your response would have been correct'. Om saw the point and agreed to use proper self-talk the next time. When these two were to play the finals of a major tournament, Om invited me to watch his game. I tried to reach in time but was held up in traffic. I could see only the last two shots. Om had crushed him in straight frames.

Three Roles of Your Mind

Doubts about the ability of your own self can arise any time and, if entertained, they can damage your performance. Imagine a court case, in which one lawyer puts forth his side of the case, the opposition lawyer argues in favour of his side. Finally, the judge considers both the sides and gives the judgement. When you are facing a challenge, your mind is playing all these three roles, that of the judge and also of both the advocates. It is your mind that raises the doubts about inadequate practice, fitness or your ability to face the particular opponent. Then the mind itself makes an attempt, mostly feeble, to argue that you can face the challenge and finally the mind only sits in judgement. If it gives a decision in favour of the doubt, you have already lost the match.

Yoga has come forth with a very powerful tool to deal with all doubts. You should develop a convincing argument in favour of your faith, dedication and abilities to face the challenge. This argument is to be used in self-talk to convince you in favour of 'I can face this challenge'.

Then half the battle is already won. After all, faith is a matter of convincing yourself. Once your mind gives a decision as the judge, in favour of your capability, you can surpass all your expectations. That is what the champions successfully keep doing time and again.

A question is usually asked, 'Are mistakes to be forgotten or glossed over?' The answer is, of course, in the negative. Mistakes have to be analysed and remedies have to be found out to drop them from your system. Then, alone, you have a chance to improve your performance. But these analysis sessions have to be planned properly and their frequency has to be controlled. As far as possible, do the analysis sessions only with your coach, who should be able to assist you in correcting your technique. If the services of the coach are not readily available, discuss the techniques with other knowledgeable persons or read about them and then do the analyses yourself. Avoid analysing your techniques with all and sundry, who hardly have any knowledge. During the analysis, care should be taken to discuss the positive points also and these sessions should be ended with a discussion about the perfect technique. If possible, after each of the analysis sessions, there should be a visualization session and the execution of the perfect technique should be visualized. Ending the discussions after description of the mistakes is very dangerous as the mistakes get accentuated and confirmed into the system.

FOCUS ON ACTION, PULL, PROPEL

Practising Self-talk

The *wani* or the power of communication plays a major role in your performance. It keeps your focus alert. All counting, measuring and awareness of time are taken care of by the *wani*. You have to be reminded of the rules and the time frame and this is the job of *wani*. It is also required for making you aware of the correct sequence to be followed and can strengthen your resolve and willpower. But when playing sports, the expression of non-verbal skills requires the *wani* to play a secondary and supporting role. Unless you train yourself to control your verbal thought processes, there is the danger of the *wani* going on babbling incessantly affecting your focus and responses adversely.

Wani also plays a major role in establishing your faith. That is why all the religions preach regular reading of scriptures, daily prayers and chanting of mantras. By doing so, you are taking charge of your verbal thought processes giving them proper direction. By regular reading and listening to thoughts expressed by knowledgeable persons you add to your knowledge, then you perfect your skill by regular practice and keep both these fresh and up-to-date by discussions with others and further practice. Daily prayer is a reminder of the direction and building up of faith. Since *wani*, by force of habit, keeps indulging in non-stop verbal thoughts, it is given the task of chanting mantras. The mind is to be trained to dwell on the meaning of the words being chanted. Then it gets into the mood to produce proper responses and the body follows every decision in perfect coordination.

When a non-verbal experience like playing a shot is being taken, *wani* plays the role of a silent observer to record the experience and to reproduce it later for the benefit of self or others. When you talk about the experience or write about it, the mind goes through the experience again. If you do this more often, it gives the same advantage as the physical practice. In verbalizing the experience, the sequence of observation, selection of the response and its actual execution are repeated in the mind and the *wani* identifies the correct verbal thoughts, which lead to that particular experience. That is why you have to limit your verbalizing of mistakes to analysis sessions only. Talk about your positive experiences and if there is nobody to listen to you, write about them. This is of great help in establishing the correct sequences and responses into your system.

Writing a diary of excellence, composing and uttering or reading daily affirmations or prayers; identifying and using correct cue phrases/words or mantras, which will lead to the proper responses are techniques of great help in controlling the verbal thought processes and building up a useful self-talk. These are dealt with in later chapters.

ACTION POINTS

- To optimize your performance, you have to train yourself to control your verbal thoughts and the responses to them.

- Doubts about the ability of your own self can arise any time and if entertained, they can damage your performance.

- As far as possible, do the analysis sessions only with your coach, who should be able to assist you in correcting your technique.

- *Wani* or the power of communication plays a major role in establishing your faith.

- When you talk about the experience or write about it, the mind goes through the experience again.

6

Visualization: Controlling Non-verbal Thoughts

Visualization is a technique of meditation that was followed in ancient India. The human mind has the capacity to go into the past and future at will and also to draw inferences about the things happening elsewhere. When the mind is exercising any of these skills, it is visualizing. Exercising the choice of focus is the key to train the mind as the habit of the mind to leave the time and space frames of the present and to wander about can cause serious problems unless controlled by regular practice. The normal trend or universal habit is to dwell only on mistakes, flaws, failures, negative occurrences, etc., of the past, present and future. This has to be curbed with a strong will and regular practice, otherwise it will lead to misery.

Practising dwelling on the best from the past, known as purification of memory, and using proper self-talk for drawing inferences and creating images of successful journey towards the goals and their actual realization are of great help. All these are exercises in visualization. Whenever verbal thoughts are entertained, they get translated into the language of non-verbal thoughts or the language of experience. This is picturization or visualization. This is a constant ongoing process and has to be controlled with a strong self-talk and regular practice of visualization.

Reinforce the Best Performance

Imagine picking up a fresh lemon and cutting a slice from it. Now just think that you are squeezing the slice into your mouth. Just as you are reading these words your mouth must have started watering. These words get visualized and the inner power produces the response of saliva in the mouth to receive the acidic lime juice. The inner power understands only the language of experience and not that of words. *Wani* and mind, therefore, keep translating all verbal thoughts into visuals. Initially, it is better to depend on words for controlling the process of visualization. But visualization without the assistance of words is more desirable, for it creates deeper impressions.

In learning non-verbal techniques required for sports, visualization plays a major role. You observe somebody playing brilliantly and get attracted to the sport. You then visualize your idol or role model performing and then mentally replace him or her by your own self. Then you start picking up the skill. That is why most of the great players leave a stamp of their style on almost all the players from that particular region.

The Russian sports psychologists made a major contribution by evolving techniques of visualization for improvement in sports performance. In the decade of 1970–80, they took the world of sports by surprise and the Russian athletes emerged as the most dominant force in sports. Charles Garfield, a leading sports psychologist from the USA has described his experience with the Russian scientists in Milan in the year 1979.

Charles Garfield refused to accept that the excellence the Russian athletes were achieving was due only to mental training. He demanded for a demonstration and agreed to carry out an experiment on himself. He had been a weightlifter earlier but had stopped serious training several years back. Just going through an intensive visualization session for two hours, he could repeat his career's best performance, which he had thought would take him several months of dedicated practice.

Even before that, the leading athletes all over the world had been making use of visualization for mentally rehearsing their performances in advance. I remember the renowned rifle shooting coach Dr Hammerl from Hungary telling us how he used visualization techniques for his performance during the Tokyo Olympics in 1964. He used to visualize a hole appearing in the centre of the target and rehearse mentally what he had to do for achieving that result. He used to repeat this procedure before every shot he fired. He shot a memorable match in the Olympics winning the gold!

Another Olympic gold medallist, Lee Evans, who won the 400 metres running gold with an Olympic and World record, at the Mexico Olympics in 1968, used to spend many hours visualizing the whole race again and again. He used to create an image in his mind as to how he would run the race in the Olympics and how his body would perform from beginning to end. He imagined every stride he would take one after another. This helped improve his timing and the world record created by him was broken only after 23 years!

Jack Nicklaus, the champion golfer, has described in his book *Golf My Way*, how he used the techniques of visualization. He writes: 'I never hit a shot, not even in practice, without having a very sharp, in-focus picture of it in my head. It's like a colour movie. First I "see" the ball where I want it to finish, nice and white and sitting up high on bright green grass. Then the scene quickly changes and I "see" the ball going there, its path, trajectory and shape, even its behaviour on landing. Then there is sort of a fade out. And the next scene shows me making the kind of swing that will turn the previous images into reality.'

Then he adds the tip, 'Just make sure your movies show a perfect shot. We don't want any horror films of shots flying into sand or water or out of bounds.'

All the top Indian sportspersons who have worked with me have been making extensive use of various techniques of visualization, which are described in the later chapters.

Purification of memory or reinforcing the best from the past, by remembering it again and again, makes a major contribution to the perfecting of a skill. Repeated physical practice of the skill in any sport is expected to build up a muscle memory of the skill. But in actual practice, the action may be correct or it may be incorrect also. Then the muscle memory built up is of mixed nature and includes incorrect responses too. Under stressful match conditions, sometimes there is the risk of the wrong response surfacing. How do you avoid this? Distinctly visualizing the correct action once it has manifested, is like again going through the experience itself. According to the science of yoga, memory and experience are one and the same. If you remember clearly and visualize the correct response repeatedly, it gives the same benefit as going through the right action over and over again. This also curbs the natural habit of focusing on wrong experiences in the past and the resultant deterioration in quality of concentration and confidence.

Similarly, whenever the mind has to go into the future, it has to go by your choice and dwell only on the possibilities you want to project before yourself. Visualizing the goals and the stages in the journey being achieved is known as *sankalpa*. Imagining wrong things happening in future is exactly the opposite of this and is known as *vikalpa*. Habit of the mind to indulge in *vikalpa* has to be broken by regular practice of *sankalpa*. Relentless positivization is recommended. If negative thoughts occur, instead of keeping the focus on them and allowing them to be visualized, the focus should be shifted to positive thoughts and a habit has to be formed to keep visualizing those.

For a non-verbal skill like sports, this is essential. Doing any intricate action like playing a stroke or propelling the body faster requires a special power known in yoga as *siddhi*. Focused repetition of the action places a demand on the system to produce the cells required for the decision and its execution to perform that action. Visualizing the best actions in the past and anticipated brilliance in the future with a sharp focus gives the same effect as actual physical practice, and the special power to execute the correct action is cultivated.

Relaxation is a precondition for all visualization exercises. Removal of all tensions from the body and mind is a must, for these tensions distract the mind, and the focus required for meditation cannot be achieved. It is advisable to visualize some familiar objects first, paying attention to the shape, size and colours. This should be followed by visualizing multiple objects such as the venue of competition, equipment to be used for the sport, group of familiar persons, and so on. Visualizing the objects of different senses separately and together is the next step. Experiencing an event involves all the senses and the mind has to be put through the practice gradually.

Familiarity of the venue is one of the most essential factors of remaining in comfort zone during a match. The inner power feels that you are safe in familiar surroundings and ensures an easy flow of the skill. That is why performance on home ground or pitch, before a familiar and favourable crowd is easy. Even while performing at a strange place, there may be a few familiar signals present. Dimensions of the court or ground, the equipment being used, the clothing one is wearing, position and actions of the umpires, etc., are all signals capable of bringing the mind into comfort zone. When performing on an unknown venue, you should look for these signals and visualize a positive response to all of them. In the regular visualization sessions, the venue and your performance with poise and focus should be visualized repeatedly, so that the uncomfortable feeling of being in a strange or potentially hostile place is taken care of.

All performances have to get a positive response at least from the well-wishers. Mostly, the negativization starts with the thought that the others are going to make fun of me or criticize me, if I fail. Then the negative thoughts get visualized and affect the performance adversely. To counter this possibility, visualize excellence in performance followed by a positive response from the well-wishers. This also reinforces the drive to excel and win.

Visualizing the achievement of the long-term and short-term goals makes the direction of efforts clear to the inner power. Actually, the nearest short-term goal or the stage of progress that you are going through needs to be visualized more often. Mere visualization of achieving long-term goals may result in daydreaming. All visualization exercises are aimed at building up faith in your own self. Daydreaming leaves place for doubts and can cause serious problems.

As regards visualization of sports skills and performance, it is necessary to understand the concept of transition points well. You should analyse your sport properly and identify the challenges that you have to face. Then you will be able to select proper visualization exercises. Doing these regularly will build up a strong system, and ensure an easy flow of skills in all conditions.

ACTION POINTS

- The habit of the mind to leave the time and space frame of the present to wander about can cause serious problems unless controlled by regular practice.

- Purification of memory or reinforcing the best from the past, by remembering it again and again, makes a major contribution to perfecting of a skill.

- According to the science of yoga, memory and experience are one and the same.

- Relaxation is a precondition for all visualization exercises.

- Visualizing the achievement of the long-term goals makes the direction of efforts clear to the inner power.

- All visualization exercises are aimed at building up faith in your own self.

7

Analysing the Game and Handling the Transition Points

For perfecting the technique required for the game chosen by you, the concepts of active and recovery phases, transition points, roles and role-shifts should be understood clearly in order to decide the type of focus required and the visualization exercises to be adopted to build up the skills. You should take the assistance of your coach for this analysis. Along with it, extensive reading of the experiences of the past and present players in the game is also recommended strongly.

I would like to mention here the experience of Devendra Joshi, a great billiards and snooker player, who has reached the finals of the World Amateur Billiards and has several brilliant performances to his credit. He was playing the 1995 World Billiards Championship in Mumbai, in excellent form. But after reaching the semifinals, he told me that he had reached an unsurmountable hurdle. He was to play Robbie Foldvari, who was a very tough opponent. Devendra, like all the Indian players, used to play a very fast game. Robbie was the exact opposite of that and played in an extremely slow tempo. Perhaps, this had worked as a good strategy for him as his opponents used to get bored and irritated, affecting their form. Devendra informed me that he had found it impossible to find a way to overcome the irritation and he had lost all the previous matches to that player.

We sat for individual discussion in a late-night session and analysed the game of billiards together. Two opponents play this game in turns. I argued that in the four-hour match, if Devendra had the chance of making 60 visits, then his opponent would be making 59, 60 or 61 visits. The maximum advantage his opponent could have was only of one visit. My point was that, the form in which Devendra was playing, his opponent in the semifinal would require at least 15 to 20 visits more to score higher than him. The habit of keeping the focus on the score and the time being lost thereof, while the opponent was playing was the main trouble. I advised Devendra to keep the focus on Foldvari's brilliance in execution of shots and the strategy of positioning for the next shot, rather than the score.

Luckily, Devendra was convinced with this argument and agreed to make serious efforts to live the roles properly in the match next day. It was one of the most memorable matches he had played or I had seen being played. Changing the habit just overnight was a very tough task. Foldvari had taken a comfortable lead in the first half. But Devendra used the proper self-talk, kept his cool and focused beautifully on his own technique when on the table and won a very close match by a difference of just about 30 odd points. It was great joy for me to see two Indians, Geet Sethi and Devendra Joshi, play the finals of the World Billiard Championships.

In billiards, the active phases come only when you are actually playing. When it is the opponent's turn, you have to shift into a role of a spectator. When your turn comes, you have to get into a player's role and handle the active phases in full focus. If you take care to separate these two roles and do not allow them to overlap, you are in a better position to control your moods and ensure an excellent flow of skills during the active phase of the game. Scores really do not matter, for the opponent cannot do anything to your game when you are at the table nor can you do anything when he is playing. Then why worry about the factors which cannot affect your game at all? Get into the habit of living the roles fully and ensuring that the moments of role-shifts separate the roles totally, and the chances of your winning improve.

Active Phase

Once you decide to take up any game seriously, analyse all the aspects of the game. Roles and role-shifts should be identified. In all team games, these role-shifts appear very fast and have to be handled carefully. In a game like football, the player has to play the role of an observer and simultaneously keep moving to be in a position to tackle or trap the ball. When he gets the chance, he has to play the role of taking control over the ball and then shift to the role of a goal scorer or passer. The focus, every moment, has to be that of living the role fully. In a volley game like tennis, these roles of an observer and performer keep appearing alternately at a very fast pace. In between, comes the phase of decision making. A very sharp and alert focus is required to execute these roles. The mind lingering on any other matter is detrimental to the performance.

Active phase is when you are actually performing and expressing your skill. Recovery phase is the time between two active phases. The gaps between two points, two games, time off and stops in the progress of the game are also recovery phases. Golf is one game in which the active phase is very short and the recovery phase is extremely long. As against that, sailing is one game in which the active phase lasts for the whole course, without any recovery phase at all. The player has to remain alert and active throughout the length of the competition. That is why, it is one of the toughest physical challenges.

Once the active and recovery phases are identified and analysed properly, the player can plan to make up for the loss of energy and shifts in strategy, if need be, during the recovery phase. In the game of billiards as discussed earlier, the opponent's visit is a long recovery phase for you, while during your visit, the active phase starts when you bend on the table for execution of the stroke and ends when you get up after your follow through. In between two active phases there is a short recovery phase before you start executing the next shot.

Your effort should be to relax and do deep breathing during the recovery phase in order to replenish the energy used up and try and focus deeply during the active phase. Recovery phase can also be used to rebuild your focus, confidence and mood by an effective self-talk. If the recovery phase is long enough, the advanced players use it also for visualization.

Recovery Phase

I was once playing a billiards league match in Mumbai. The opponent was slightly better than me and it was very important for me to win my tie for giving our team any chance to win the match. In the initial stages, the opponent got an alarmingly large number of flukes. I was getting irritated and broke down on some easy shots. During the recovery phases of my opponent's visit, I used an effective self-talk and convinced myself that the opponent was not playing well since he was missing the strokes played and that was how he was getting the flukes. As against that, I was playing in good form and getting my strokes and positions correctly. I, therefore, had every chance of winning. This convincing self-talk helped me bridge the gap by a good brake in the closing moments and I managed to win the game by just one point, and became the hero for that day.

The concept of transition points has to be grasped very well, for it is extremely useful for building up the skill flow. Transition point is one in which there is a sudden change in movement, speed or direction. Every move has several transition points and regular practice polishes them well. Real skill in any sport is handling these transition points accurately at the precise moment. In yoga, this skill is referred to as *siddhi* or a special power. By regular physical practice, the skill to handle these points has to be built up and then, it should be reinforced into the system by frequent visualization. Then the system knows that it should reproduce the cells required for the sharp observation, proper selection of the response and its actual execution. The correct responses keep appearing naturally and a flow of the skill is ensured. The champions have this *siddhi* and that is why there is grace in their movements, which makes their game so attractive to watch.

Imagine an athlete preparing for a long jump. He is standing there preparing mentally for the execution of the jump. The first transition point comes when he starts moving from the stationary position. Every step he takes in gathering speed and positioning for the final take-off is a transition point. The final take-off is the most important transition point for the building up of which all the earlier movements are being done. He takes off into the air and lands on the feet, which is the final transition point. In the air also, the movements aimed at assisting the body being propelled through air have several transition points—these also have to be taken carefully to land properly. All these transition points have to be identified and whenever taken correctly, should be ingrained into the system by repeated visualization.

In the chapters dealing with specific types of games, these concepts are dealt with in further details.

ACTION POINTS

- Analyse all the aspects of your game carefully.

- Identify all the challenges and different roles you have to play. Make sure that you play every role fully. Take care to handle the role-shifts well.

- An active phase is when you are actually performing and expressing your skill. A recovery phase is the time between two active phases.

- A recovery phase can also be used to rebuild your focus, confidence and mood by an effective self-talk.

- A transition point is the one in which there is a sudden change in movement, speed or direction.

8

Concentration and Attention-Focus

Billiards World Championship finals were being played in Mumbai in 1992. Geet Sethi was playing one of his toughest opponents, Mike Russell of England, and was on a big break. A number of times he had to stop playing because of commotion in the hall as some dignitary would walk in. Once he crossed the 500 mark, a few newcomers applauded loudly. He looked up and had an eye contact with them and acknowledged the applause. Again, he dived deep into concentration and scored a break of over 800 and won the match comfortably. His ability of achieving the required depth of concentration was just exemplary.

Suma Shirur, Anjali Bhagwat and Avneet Kaur Siddhu, the top rifle shooters in India, have achieved the feat of shooting the perfect score of 400/400 in major competitions. That means hitting a small dot equal to the full stop in this book at a distance of 10 metres, 40 times in a row. They have mastered the skill of focusing for every shot and achieving the desired result.

Another example is the master batsman Rahul Dravid. His ability to live in the present and to take care of one ball at a time, even against heavy odds is simply fantastic. With the sharp attention-focus he has developed, he did an excellent job as a makeshift wicketkeeper for the Indian cricket team, and as a fielder has taken the maximum number of catches in test matches. Batting skill in cricket is known for its glorious uncertainties, because of the sudden death rule. Just one mistake and you are back in the pavilion. As a batsman, he has earned the title of 'The Wall' being the most dependable batsman.

Keep the Focus on What Is Happening

All these great players have become legends in their lifetime. They have cultivated the art of sharp attention-focus and living in the particular moment and producing the correct responses in spite of the pressure of emerging the best in various conditions. This requires continuous hard and sincere work over the period of years. Body, mind and the power of communication known as *wani* are the three instruments available for a player to excel in any sport. A perfect coordination in these three is essential for any sports skill. First, physical fitness has to be developed and then it is to be converted into the skill that is required for the specific sport, by regular practice. Similarly, the ability to concentrate and maintain a sharp attention-focus has to be cultivated by specific basic exercises and then that ability has to be converted into the skill of producing the desired responses by visualizing regularly.

Do Not Focus on What Is Going to Happen

The mind has the power of leaving the time and space frame of the present and moving about at will anywhere in space or in the past or future. Then *wani* tries to function on its own and indulges in verbal thoughts, which can disturb the attention-focus. Keeping the mind and *wani* together is the first task. Luckily, the body always remains in present.

Yoga teaches you to link all your verbal and non-verbal thought processes with the body, to come into the present. This is the beginning of concentration. Then the attention-focus has to be shifted to what is happening and the role which you have to play. A sharp attention-focus requires the involvement of all the five senses, the mind, and *wani*.

Focus on Breathing, Focus on the Ball

Breathing is a continuous process and comparatively easy to focus on. Every incoming breath brings fresh energy into the system and each outgoing breath carries away the waste in the system. Since this process is taking place without a single break in the present, focus on breathing brings the mind also into the present. By force of habit, the mind keeps going into the past and broods on the mistakes and failures. Then, with a foul mood and damaged self-image, it looks into the future and keeps worrying about the outcome of events to come, and entertains doubts about the ability to deal with them. This generates fear and loss of control over the senses. Then further mistakes start occurring and the emotions of anger and frustration take charge of your mind. Most of the stress in your life is a result of this continuous negative activity indulged into by the mind.

By bringing the focus on breathing, two immediate results are achieved. Your mind comes into the present, breaking the chain of reactions mentioned earlier. It also makes you aware of your link with the Universal Energy known in yoga as prana. This link can restore the confidence in your own self. You, then, come out of the debilitating grief about the past and also the fear about the future. It is, then, possible for you to take care of the challenge you are facing in the present. The stress of handling a challenge becomes much more manageable and your performance level improves automatically.

The wandering habit of the mind is not easy to break. You may bring the focus on breathing, but it is not easy to maintain it unless you make it a point to practise it regularly. Coming into the present by focusing on breath is one of the best habits to be cultivated. That marks the beginning of concentration. For the type of focus required for every sport, you will have to learn to shift the attention-focus from other thought processes to breathing and then shift it to the situation, your role and the technique. Sporting skills require the attainment of deep focus during the active phase and living in every moment of that phase. All the main transition points occur during the active phase and the focus has to be sharp enough to handle them all accurately at the precise moment. Such focus takes care of all role-shifts. The strategy to take care of sudden challenges also unfolds itself promptly. The flow of skill is ensured and chances of winning improve. The focus achieved during the active phase has to be followed through into the initial moments of the recovery phase. Otherwise the mind, which is eager to find out the result of every action, gives up control over the technique and a mistake is likely to occur.

Unless the habit of remaining focused on the technique is formed by regular practice and visualization, the mind starts wandering in the recovery phase and this mood continues in the active phase also. Keeping the mind focused requires effort and energy. You do not require the same depth of focus for the whole period of the match or competition. Another habit of defocusing during the recovery phase should be formed by focusing on breathing towards the end of it and shifting the focus to the object or technique as soon as the active phase starts. The recovery phase can also be used for relaxing, replenishing the energy reserves by deep breathing, and rebuilding the self-image and concentration through effective self-talk.

Sporting skills requiring physical activity are essentially non-verbal. Decision making is done by the mind during these movements. But the *wani*, which controls the verbal thought processes, has the habit of going on with the self-talk. This habit has to be curbed. *Wani* does have a role to play by taking care of the time factor and the correct sequences in the expression of skills and also for drawing inferences about the opponent's strategy. But this is only a supporting role. It has to surrender the dominating role to the mind. That is why the chanting of mantras or cue words and phrases has been given so much of importance in yoga. The player and team coach should analyse the best performances together. The verbal thought processes, which have helped the correct responses to come out, should also be identified. Then they will be in a position to find out the mantras which may be used only if required. The deep urge of *wani* to keep saying something is satisfied this way and the thoughts leading to correct actions are introduced in the system.

It should be understood clearly that the cue words or phrases serve only as props to enter deeper concentration required for the sports skill. As the skill and its expression get perfected, the words drop out automatically and the level of performance improves further. But you should not fight shy of using them if needed, as they ensure the correct responses, which are so essential for winning.

The sequence of observation, selection of response and its actual execution requires a very sharp focus. The process of building this focus starts with Pranayama, which according to yoga, qualifies you to start concentration. The next step is to practise focusing on stationary objects and concentrating deeply while observing an event. All movements involve changes in positions and are therefore considered as events. The final steps are the regular physical practice of the sport, visualization of transition points and the part to be played by you. All these steps, once built into your regular practice schedules, will help you develop the type of focus required for the sport you have chosen.

For the deep, sharp focus essential for sports, the dedication, drive, faith in your capacities and proper mood are vital factors. Effort should be directed to build up a muscle memory, which will automatically keep bringing the correct responses to the signals in the course of the events. The *wani* remains busy in reminding one of the rules, the time factor, the sequence of events, and provides proper arguments to ward off doubts and distractions. Whenever there is a loss of focus, concentration on breathing and then making the technique of dealing with the situation the centre of attention, ensure the easy flow of skill. Past glory or the chance of realizing the goal can also become strong distractions and spoil the focus.

Bringing the mind to the present, and keeping the body, mind and *wani* perfectly coordinated guarantee a consistent high-level performance.

ACTION POINTS

- The body, the mind and the power of communication known as *wani* are the three instruments available for a player to excel in any sport.

- Yoga teaches you to link all your verbal and non-verbal thought processes with the body, to come to the present.

- Coming to the present by focusing on breath is one of the best habits to be cultivated.

- Defocus during the recovery phase. Focus on breathing towards the end of that phase. Shift the focus to the object or your technique in the active phase. These are some of the best habits to cultivate.

- Bringing the mind in the present, and keeping the body, mind and *wani* perfectly coordinated guarantee a consistent high-level performance.

9

Relaxation, Rest and Letting Go

In my early college days, we had the chance of watching Garfield Sobers in action. He was our hero in international cricket. Every movement of his on the field appeared full of grace. Tiger Woods, the golfing legend, also exuded a similar charm when playing at the top of his form. This grace is the personal property of champions. They are confident about their ability to face any challenge. Their body movements reflect confidence. There are no unnecessary tensions in the muscles. When you are using the muscles, they get tensed up momentarily and then these are expected to relax again. Once you have perfected the skill required for your game and the confidence of using it, you get this ability to use only the muscles required for the action, keeping the rest of the body relaxed, which brings grace in all the movements. Such charm in sports like gymnastics and diving has given them a lot of spectator-value, for it is very pleasing to watch the flow of movements.

Confidence and relaxation go together, while tension and fear go together. A person who is not confident about his abilities cannot relax. Tensions and fears in the mind get transmitted to the body and the movements no longer resemble those of a champion. A higher level of confidence helps you relax and if you learn the skill of relaxation, the level of confidence automatically improves.

Confidence Brings Grace to Movement

Imagine a person learning to swim. He is afraid of leaving the side of the pool and tries to be as near the side rail as possible. The fear of drowning is supreme in his mind. He cannot relax the muscles of his body and all his movements are awkward. He exerts much more than the good swimmer, but covers only a short distance before he grabs the rail again. Once he gets the confidence of not drowning and finds the correct movements to propel his body forward, letting go of the rail is no more a problem. He is confident and there is no unnecessary tension in his mind or body. The proper muscle tone required for a swimmer is easily achieved and the movements become graceful. Less exertion is now required to propel the body through water.

The fear of failure has a similar effect on the sportsman. His whole body tenses up and a tense body gets exhausted very soon. Tensions in the mind do not allow him to relax and use up the energy reserves fast. The resultant feeling of fatigue affects his decision making and also the performance. Repeated physical practice gives the player confidence of executing the skills properly and unnecessary tensions in the body start disappearing. Just as the learning of skill in swimming reduces the fear of drowning, perfecting the skill required by regularly practising it and getting the match experience, reduce the fear of losing. Then the action starts acquiring grace as the working muscles also tense up as and when required and then relax again.

Strength, stamina and correct responses required for the expression of skill in any game are all stored in the cells of your body. When you use your senses and the body for the movements required in the sport in practice sessions or in a match, you are placing an order to your system as to what types of cells it has to build up. These cells are formulated during the period of sleep and rest. These two factors are, therefore, as important as the physical practice itself. If you try to follow very hectic schedules in the hope of improvement, the system will have no time to reproduce the cells and build up the energy lost. You tend to overstrain whenever a major competition is approaching. Actually it is advisable to preserve the energy reserves rather than getting fatigued.

Relaxation is an art, which has to be learned through constant dedicated practice. Your system has to learn how to let go and relax totally, when you are not indulging in any activity. Even remembering the past activity or anticipating the activity in future tire you out. Stopping physical activity does not necessarily stop the mental activity. Your mind also has to stop its activity and cooperate in the attempt to relax. Continued mental activity causes increase in anxiety level and does not allow you to relax physically. You need to cultivate the art of total dedicated relaxation to get proper sleep and rest so that the required skills, strength and stamina are built up in your system.

While actually playing also, relaxation has a major role to play. It stops the wastage of energy and the energy reserves last longer since they are used quite economically. This skill to relax while on the move has to be perfected in the practice sessions. During the active phase of the game you need to practise relaxing all the non-working muscle groups. Then in the recovery phase the working muscle groups have to learn to relax to the maximum possible extent.

Terry Orlick, the famous sports psychologist from the USA has pointed out that jaw muscles and the shoulder muscles have a habit of tensing up unnecessarily and special attention should be paid to relax them. Even the working muscles have a tendency to remain tensed up for some time even beyond the active phase. It is advisable for the player to identify the muscle groups in the body, which become tense when not needed and the working muscle groups, which have a tendency to remain tense even after the task is over. Then in practice sessions, these groups have to be trained to relax.

Sleep is the best means of relaxation. It builds up the lost energy reserves and removes fatigue from the system. Resisting the force of gravity causes most of the tensions in the body. While indulging in any activity like walking, running, climbing a hill or even while sitting down you are offering resistance to the gravitational pull. If you lie down, no muscle tone is required in the body and relaxation starts making it possible for you to go to sleep. Your conscious mind loses control and the subconscious takes over. It, then, does the work of replenishing the lost energy and building up the energy reserves. Such sleep rejuvenates you and you wake up fresh.

But the mind is sometimes reluctant to stop thinking and clings to the imaginary supports and refuses to let go. Then it becomes impossible to sleep. You just lie down but the quality of rest is poor and the task of replenishing the energy lost during an activity is not fulfilled properly. As a result you spend the time in bed without sleep and get up feeling more anxious and fatigued than you were at the time of retiring. Light walks or swims, massages, tub baths and showers, walking in a darkish room for a few paces, a very light snack or a glass of warm milk are all useful aids to fall asleep. Watching a TV programme, a movie or reading a book are good means of relaxing but they activate the thought processes and are not recommended just prior to retiring.

In a car, the combustion of fuel takes place only in the engine. In your body it is stored and burnt also all over. This burning produces the energy required for activity, whether mental or physical. The waste created in this process of burning has to be thrown out of the system. Then the energy along with the reserves has to be replenished for future use. All this process involves a mind-boggling workload and is constantly going on in our body with the efficiency of a well-run large-scale industry. This becomes possible because of prana, the power entering our body through every breath. This power controls the digestive and the circulo-respiratory systems. It is responsible for the functioning of all our senses. Rest and relaxation are essential for effective use of the prana energy and for preserving it in the body for future use.

Shavasana, Yoga Nidra and Nyasa are some of the best techniques in Yoga for effective relaxation.* Shifting the focus of thoughts on pleasant memories; actually visualizing the best experiences from the past; visualizing confidence and poise in future events; building up faith in your abilities to face challenges by means of an effective self-talk; remaining in the present by keeping the focus

---

* Details about Shavasana and Yoga Nidra can be available on any good book on yogasanas. But the technique of Nyasa is followed only by a certain sect of yogis and I have not come across its detailed description in any text. I have, therefore, added a separate chapter on it giving whatever I have learnt from knowledgeable persons and the way in which we have been practising it. I found it to be the most beneficial for sportsmen as it can be done even during the activity and has the additional advantage of keeping you in the present. If you make the effort of perfecting the technique of Nyasa, the benefits are numerous in all walks of life, and I recommend it very strongly.

on breathing are also very useful exercises to build up the skill of relaxation. You should include any one or all of these in your daily schedules for learning and perfecting the art of relaxation. Once practised well, you can use those techniques to relax your system whenever there are unscheduled breaks in the training or the matches, like travelling or waiting for your match to be called, etc.

ACTION POINTS

- Confidence and relaxation go together, while tension and fear go together.

- Repeated physical practice gives the player confidence of executing the skills properly, and unnecessary tensions in the body disappear.

- One needs to cultivate the art of total dedicated relaxation to get proper sleep and rest so that the required skills, strength and stamina are built up in one's system.

- Sleep is the best means of relaxation.

- Shavasana, Yoga Nidra and Nyasa are some of the best techniques in yoga for effective relaxation.

10

Coping with Distractions and Adversities

The toughest part of any achievement is the handling of distractions and adverse conditions. Everyone feels enamoured by the glittering success achieved by top sportsmen. But how many are aware of the sacrifices, sufferings and the sustained efforts made by them to acquire the skills, and maintain high levels of performance? The position of a hero in sports is not enviable at all, for he has to bear a heavy cross of expectations which include that of others too. A closer look at the biographies of all the greats in sports will reveal numerous instances of handling distractions and miserably adverse conditions.

In 1999, the legendary hero in cricket, Sachin Tendulkar had to rush back from the World Cup matches in England to attend his father's funeral. There was a very close bond between the father and son and it must have been extremely difficult for Sachin to endure the shock of grief. But he returned to England and in the very next match, scored a superb century. It is no wonder that he is simply adored by the millions who are his fans.

A female rifle shooter who was leaving for the 1996 Olympics along with her 17-day-old daughter was deserted by her boyfriend. This shock came as she was about to leave for the Olympics venue. She carried her infant daughter along, continued her training and won the gold medal in the Olympics.

The biography of Lance Armstrong, the great athlete who has won the 'Tour De France', the most gruelling long-distance cycling race as many as seven times, that too after fighting against cancer, makes very inspiring reading. It should inspire you to undergo the suffering required to reach your goals. Staying away from things you like and doing things well even if you do not like them are the real challenges in life.

There is a tale about Emperor Akbar and his wisest and cleverest courtier Birbal. Once, while walking along a river bank, the Emperor drew a line in the sand with his stick and challenged his courtiers to make it small without touching it. After all the courtiers failed, Birbal came forward and with his stick drew a longer line. Automatically the earlier line became smaller.

You have several different roles to play in your life. All of them are very important for you and you cannot afford to fail in any of them. If you do, your performance in all the spheres can deteriorate. Then there will be a large number of things which you would love to do, but have not been able to because of your commitments. Thoughts about your other roles and the strong desire to have the things you want act as magnets and draw you away from the sphere of performance. Then the focus is lost and mistakes start occurring. All of a sudden, you find yourself performing much below your level.

You will have to play a trick like the cleverest of the clever, Birbal. You should have a more powerful magnet with you than all these magnets put together. Then their power to distract you gets weakened and you remain in control.

As per the science of yoga, desires are unlimited. They are present in the human mind largely in miniscule forms like seeds. Whenever the conditions are favourable, these seeds germinate and we notice these desires. They are suppressed if it is not convenient for us to fulfil them. If the desires are very strong, or we feel that there is no harm in fulfilling them, efforts are made to satisfy those desires. Suppressed desires can cause a lot of harm to our personality. The better method is to weaken these desires so that they lose power over us and go back to the seed form. Yoga recommends building up the discipline from within. This requires sustained, unceasing effort. The focus should be on weakening the desires and not on suppressing them. Then remaining in control is no more a problem. Feeling of satiation should be developed whenever the desires are fulfilled and the thought processes have to be controlled by constant training and self-talk.

The inner faculties, together referred to as the mind, need to be trained in keeping away from distractions. Merely keeping the body and senses deprived of the things of their liking does not help. If your mind is convinced that the particular desires are causing you damage, it can, then, successfully combat the craving and the distraction becomes weak. This is where inspiring thoughts from the experience of great sports achievers are of tremendous help.

You already have the magnet, which can prove to be stronger than all the outside distractions. That is your will power. It can be strengthened by the discipline of following your schedules meticulously and by guiding your thought processes properly. It, then, successfully wards off not only distractions, but also helps you in facing adversities.

No adversity can deter a champion. This is the main difference between champions and the good players. Conditions are always going to remain adverse. A number of challenges will be thrown at you all of a sudden. Things will keep going wrong. If you are going to wait for the conditions to improve, waiting is what you will be doing. Opportunities will keep slipping off and you will not be able to achieve anything.

There will always be a large number of factors, which are not in your control. The general tendency is to go on complaining, criticizing, being bitter and losing form as a result. Adversarial feelings against anything affect your ability to focus, and even the will to perform starts diminishing. Irritation, frustration, anger, annoyance are all feelings which lead you astray. They weaken the urge to fight. Instead, you will be gripped by the thoughts of quitting. In any case, there is hardly any point in continuing with the effort if you have already given up the fight. You must always remember that *winners never quit and quitters never win*.

The habit of trying to find excuses for poor performance is the root cause for this evil. It keeps your focus only on things and happenings over which you have no control. How are your real skills, your true worth, going to be tested unless the conditions are against you? By focusing on these factors, you allow your mood to get spoiled, your perception capacity gets reduced, the choice of responses and everything else goes wrong. Ask yourself a simple question. How can you be a champion, if you perform only under favourable conditions? When everything is going wrong, you should try and control only one vital factor, that is, your own response. If you keep your focus on the negatives, the adversities, and factors totally beyond your control, you are sure to lose form. You will, then, feel surprised at the wrong responses which keep on occurring.

For all those who are keen on achievement, in any field, I would like them to read Dr Viktor Frankl's *Man's Search for Meaning*. It describes his experiences in the German concentration camps during the Second World War. He, his kith and kin suffered the worst kind of atrocities at the hands of their tormentors. Dr Frankl did not allow the physical pain to reach his mind. He could develop such a mental strength that all the inmates in the concentration camps kept coming to him for support. Finally, even the tormentors came to him for advice as to how to live with the sins weighing on their mind. The conditions described by him are worse than any imagination of Hell. But the courage with which Dr Frankl and some of his friends faced the adversities was something commendable. If you read the book, their courage will inspire you to face adverse conditions in the path of your goals. You will feel ashamed to complain of adversities.

In *Chandogya Upanishad,* a practice is prescribed for maintaining mental balance against all adversities. For this practice you have to commit yourself:

- to become forgiving and have a large heart;
- not to criticize the sun for being hot;
- not to condemn the clouds for raining;
- not to foul your mood by talking adversely about the season, weather and climate;
- not to condemn other people for not rising to your expectations;
- not to get irritated over the behaviour of other animals and not to criticize them; and
- to imagine yourself in place of all these.

Then you will realize that they are doing their job. You will not be able to change them or their behaviour. Then why allow your performance to get affected by these factors, which you will never be able to control? In short, if you want the world around you to improve, it is not going to happen. If you allow an adversarial attitude to develop, no one else except you will be the loser.

Improve yourself, control your response, then the chances of winning will be the best. Your success will leave a better impact on the world than all the curses you may keep uttering.

ACTION POINTS

- The toughest part of any achievement is the handling of distractions and adverse conditions.

- Yoga recommends building up the discipline from within.

- Adversity does not deter champions.

- Winners never quit and quitters never win.

- Adversarial feelings against anything affect your ability to focus, and even the will to perform starts diminishing.

11

Thoughts, Emotions and Moods

Competitive sports require you to perform better than the opponents. You cannot win unless you get into the habit of excelling every time you play a match, or participate in a competition. No one knows how well the opponent is going to play. You have to commit yourself to doing your best no matter who your opponents are.

Emotions and moods play a major role in your ability to perform. Your desire to win the trophy and the resultant rewards make you so obsessive that you lose the focus on the skill. Competitive sports need a sharp focus on what is happening and what you are doing. If this focus is lost, mistakes start occurring; they fill your mind with the feeling of sorrow or sadness. You start getting annoyed and frustrated. You see the opportunities slipping away from your grip and you start getting doubtful about your future. Then you are afraid of losing and its consequences. You suffer all the pangs of a prisoner in a concentration camp and start wondering, 'Why am I doing this?' The idea of quitting becomes powerful. And finally you give up, trying to bask in the glory of whatever you have achieved so far.

Life is for joy! Why do you want to convict yourself and suffer? Yoga has listed several obstacles in the path of building up and using the power to focus, namely, physical or mental sickness, lethargy, doubts, neglect of required efforts, laziness and inability to control the distraction of insatiable desires, and so on. Then your dreams make you develop a mistaken notion about the level you have reached. But when the challenge is to be faced, you realize that you have not reached the level or have not been able to maintain it. You feel miserable. The energy and will to do anything is lost. You lose control over your body and senses; even the process of breathing becomes laboured.

The solution offered for getting rid of all these problems is surprisingly simple. The practice of focusing on a single element ensures that these problems disappear and they do not recur. Even if they do, they are not strong enough to deter you from the path of progress. Prana is the element that can easily be kept into focus and is strongly recommended. Besides being very easy to focus on, it brings and keeps you in the present. Then the sorrows of the past and the fears of the future cannot take a grip on you. Anger and frustration also lose their power and you develop the habit of concentrating on what you are doing rather than what has happened or what is going to happen.

If you inculcate this habit of coming and remaining in the present, you start feeling the joy of remaining in command and the real pleasure of performing at the top of your form. This is the flow of skill you will have to achieve. Winning becomes just a habit.

Now, you will have to remember that your thought processes affect your emotions and moods. You will have to cultivate the habit of monitoring your thoughts. Be careful about what you read, hear or contemplate. Allowing the mind to get involved with any kind of thought that comes across is very dangerous. That habit will lead to strengthening the problems and not your capacity to face them. Think in minute details about the skills required for your sport, read about them, go to experts in the field and listen to them, experiment with the changes in approach, style, response suggested and accept into your system whatever suits you.

For becoming a champion you need to be a very sensitive person. Feel sorry for your mistakes, but do not stay sad. Feel angry by all means but try and forgive yourself and others as quickly as possible. Do not lose control over your temper. Look to the future with curiosity about the outcome of your experiments and performance. Never take your level of skill for granted. You will have to keep on making improvisations in your skill to suit the conditions in which you are performing.

One of my coaches used to say that you are not recruited into any sport by force. You are supposed to enjoy playing and not suffer it. Playing for reward and recognition instead of the joy of excellence will soon lower your ability to perform and bring misery.

Competitive sport calls for being ruthless in the expression of your skills and not with your opponents. Hating your opponent, feeling jealous of his skills, poise and achievement are natural feelings. But they have to be controlled by cultivating the feeling of fraternity for all those who play your sport. Instead of allowing the base emotion of jealousy to take control of your mind you should be curious as to how the person performs. Focus on his excellence will reveal his secrets to you, and his skills can certainly be a part of your expertise.

Interpersonal relations are the root cause of some of the problems in handling our emotions. Though they will be dealt with separately, in greater details later, it is better to consider them here also. Yoga gives a very simple method of making use of interpersonal relations to develop your own personality. It requires you to make friends with the happiness of others; develop compassion for their sorrows; cultivate a feeling of joy in their merit and achievements and a feeling of neglect towards their sins and mistakes. This practice helps you to develop a proper attitude towards others. Then you do not fall prey to base instincts like jealousy and your focus does not get distracted because of the behaviour of others.

Sometimes, the mood and will to play is lost because of fatigue and having used up all the energy reserves. Just breathing out and holding the lungs empty for a short while takes care of that feeling. Subsequent breath is automatically drawn deeper and the energy replenishing takes place at a faster rate. Then the mood to fight back and perform better also reappears. Stress of the desire to do well and the possibility of a failure tend to tighten your chest muscles. Conscious emptying out of the lungs removes the tension from these muscles and with the subsequent incoming breath brings more fresh energy, adding to your confidence.

Meditating on the expression of the skill achieved in the past is also of great help. The focus, free flow of skill and pure joy experienced during the event in the past is brought back to memory. Your mood, then, undergoes a sea change and you can start to fight back. Meditating on the pure excellence expressed by your role models also has a similar effect. An experience of joy in any field of your liking can also be chosen as object of focus for meditation. It also has the strength of building up your mood and will to perform.

The emotions of anger, sorrow and fear have the power of driving away all the strength from your system. They lead to the mood of frustration, depression and debilitate you totally. You will, then, find it difficult to do your routine chores also. Then how will you be able to execute the complicated skills required for competitive sports?

These emotions have to be controlled by giving strength to counter feelings. The will to perform and curiosity about the future are also a part of your basic instincts. So is the emotion of compassion and the ability to forgive. All these are supposed to be the divine traits in your personality. Their careful cultivation takes care of the negative emotions of sorrow, fear and anger. It is not easy to achieve but an effort in that direction will also give you great results.

If this effort is ceaseless and dedicated, you start getting control over your emotions and moods. Then you can reach very high levels in the skills required for your sport. Without doubt, your performance level will also remain high. As a sportsperson what more should you want?

ACTION POINTS

- Emotions and moods play a major role in your ability to perform.
- Life is for joy!
- Prana is the element that can be easily kept into focus for remaining in good mood to face a challenge.
- Competitive sport calls for being ruthless in the expression of your skills and not with your opponents.
- The yoga method requires you to make friends with the happiness of others; develop compassion for their sorrows; cultivate a feeling of joy in their merit and achievements and a feeling of forgiveness towards their sins and mistakes.
- An experience of joy in any field of your liking can be chosen as the object of focus for meditation.

12

Interpersonal Relations

One of the top players in the country had shifted to another state. She played a leading role in defeating the team from her earlier state in the interstate national championships. Some journalists questioned her about her feelings on beating her own team, with which she had been playing earlier. She replied that she was happy about winning like any other time. In her interaction with the press, she criticized the earlier state administration for not being responsive to the needs of sportspersons. Her remarks were bloated out of proportion and even editorials were written about her ingratitude and negative attitude. She made an attempt to clarify what she had said and why, but her side did not get proper projection and she went through a lot of mental agony, which affected her form and performance for some time.

Top sportspersons have to learn the skill of handling the media well. They need all the positive publicity they may get. But some casual remarks can cause controversies and a lot of avoidable suffering. In the case of youngsters, their parents and coaches should give this factor a lot of thought and even train them in proper handling of the press. General experience shows that their best performances do not get the deserved attention, but some mistake made in interaction with the press gets headlines, and then the players come to considerable grief.

Such issues can cause major setbacks in their careers, create problems with the fan-following, sponsors and even the employers.

Not only with the press, a sports achiever has to be careful about all the relations. In life one has to play several roles—one in your family, one in the school, college or the workplace, one in your group of friends and once you start shining in the sport chosen, your sponsors and the employers also become vital factors to be considered. In none of these roles can you afford to fail. Failure in one role affects the focus and performance in all the other fields. Granted, that it is a difficult challenge to succeed everywhere, but the attempt should be made to do just that.

Then the roles keep shifting and also keep overlapping. Because of the speed with which these roles keep changing, it becomes all the more tough to live each role separately. You have to fix the priorities, and these will also not be of permanent nature. By choosing sports as a career, you are adding an additional factor to make heavy demands on your time and attention. In your early life, when you are expected to study and qualify for a good career in some field, sports keep drawing you away from studies. You have to put in extra hours of work, sacrificing your time and attention, which could have been spent very comfortably, enjoying your diversions. Then, that is the phase of your life when you get attracted to the other sex and the urge to choose a permanent life partner becomes predominant. That urge plays havoc with the priorities fixed, till then.

The urge to have a career, which will give you a permanent income to lead a comfortable life is also very powerful, and uncertainty in that field affects your focus, confidence and the ability to perform. According to the Upanishads, the first 24 years of your life should be spent in acquiring knowledge and skills, which will equip you to earn a good livelihood and serve the society for the rest of your life. The future, during this period, will remain uncertain and you have to learn the art of getting involved fully with whatever you are doing at that particular moment. The roles, role-shifts and the priorities should be ingrained into your system by regular practice. If you are choosing sports as a career, perfection of various skills, getting the required strength and stamina and obtaining as much experience of competition as possible must be the top priority. But that does not mean that you should neglect your studies. The habit of strictly following the timetable set by you, and living every role as fully as possible is of great help.

It is highly essential to develop your intrinsic values as a sports achiever. Achievement never comes as a fluke, you will have to invest your whole life for the gold medal or the trophy you are dreaming of. Flukes may help you once in a while, but it is highly dangerous to depend on them. Most dependable factors for any achievement are the qualities and skills built up over the years. And the skill to establish and maintain good interpersonal relations is as important as the skill required for the sport itself.

Parents and coaches have to play major roles in this particular development. Whenever this part has been neglected, players have suffered a lot of miseries. A number of them have given up in disgust, without reaching anywhere near their potential. Developing the feeling of fraternity should get maximum attention. When actually competing, an all-out effort must be made to excel and beat all opponents. But the moment competitions are over, the rivalry should also be over and good cordial relations must be developed with all the players. Actually sports offer the best opportunity to build up a player's personality. Once the national championships and the selection trials are over, all the players, who had participated till recently with so fierce a rivalry, become members of the same national team and have to perform as such. Alternating the roles of opponents and partners in glory is a very stiff challenge and unless it is faced squarely, individual glory will not be possible.

Parents of young, talented players have to pay serious attention to ensure that their child learns to handle the interpersonal relations and the role-shifts properly. They will have to bear in mind that children learn more by observation than what is taught to them by word of mouth. If the parents are bringing home worries and problems from the workplace and spoiling relations in the family, the child will pick up the same traits. By only focusing on results, it becomes very difficult for a sportsperson to maintain good relations with persons whom you have lost to or beaten. In most of the cases, the parents themselves pay so much importance to winning, that their children start thinking that parental love is conditional and will be available only if they win. This affects their psyche and the ability to focus on the task on hand, which is to play well. The parents keep forgetting that all the trophies awarded in age-group matches are only consolation prizes to encourage the children to play further and become real champions by winning the competitions in open category.

Avoid Losing Temper

Another problem that enthusiastic parents create is that they assume the role of a coach and they start verbally condemning the coaches in the presence of the children. Sometimes they take over the task and spoil the chances of the child to become a winner. If one of the parents has played the game their child has taken up, then it is all the more difficult to train the budding champion. Such parents take the responsibility to teach the coach and their children develop a poor opinion about the coach. It becomes very difficult to learn anything, for the doubts created in the mind make the skill or the knowledge being taught by the coach unacceptable to the system of the player.

Uncontrolled Temper Ruins Performance

In anticipation of having a share in the future glory, some of the coaches become too possessive about the players training under them. Actually a player becomes a champion mainly because of his ability to take decisions and to take responsibility for them. If he is expected to look outside the field of performance for the decisions to come, he will be in a very ridiculous situation, and it will be a miracle if he wins. The coach–pupil relation becomes very fruitful if the coach encourages the player to think and learn from whatever sources he can. As the player becomes accomplished, a lot of people come forth to give him advice. Part of it may be useful, while some of it may have been given with the intention of misleading him. The player should be taught by his coach to be careful with such tips and accept only what proves to be useful.

Focus on excellence and willingness to give appreciation and praise, wherever possible, is the best way to build up interpersonal relations. Caring for others, feeling sorry for their misery and sharing their joy are also good habits and make you acceptable everywhere. It becomes easier for you to focus on your skill and express it under challenging conditions, if you are popular. If you make the efforts for building and maintaining proper interpersonal relations in all the roles you have to play, the chances of your remaining focused and winning improve considerably. Why not give it a try?

ACTION POINTS

- Proper interpersonal relations in all the roles one plays improve one's chances of remaining focused and winning.
- Special efforts are needed to handle interpersonal relations, but they are very rewarding.

- The habit of strictly following the timetable set by one and living every role as per schedule, as fully as possible, is of great help.

- Alternating the roles of opponents and partners in glory is a very stiff challenge, and unless it is faced squarely, individual glory will not be possible.

- The parents of young talented players have to pay serious attention to ensure that their children learn to handle interpersonal relations and the role-shifts properly.

- The coach–pupil relation becomes very fruitful if the coach encourages the player to think and learn from whatever sources he can.

13

Teamwork and Leadership

Cricket lovers all over the world were in for a shock
in October 2005, when Ricky Ponting's Australia, the
world-champion team, took on the World XI consisting of
big legendary names in international cricket. England had
just shown that the Aussies can be beaten, by winning the
Ashes series. But the Australian cricketers made a remark-
able comeback by beating the World XI comfortably in
both the longer and shorter versions of the game.

There is a general impression that great players
thrown together will be a very tough team to face. All selectors are expected to do justice to their jobs by choosing
those players who are in the best form. There is no doubt
that any team should have the most competent players
available. But what criteria do the selectors have, except
to go by the individual performances as per the latest
records? Yet, for victory, the team needs something more
than a group of good players. They should be willing to
merge and blend their individual excellence into group
effort and work for a common goal.

The urge to excel is natural in everyone, while the skill to merge in a group has to be acquired and cultivated. Not only the player, but the parents and coaches also have a very important role to play in this aspect. They mostly tend to support and encourage individual excellence. In the process of selection, whether for inclusion in representative teams or for jobs and sponsorships, maximum weightage is given to the performance record. As such, the ability to cope with the demands of performing for the team gets neglected at all stages. Team work, so essential for top performance, in both individual and team games, does not get due attention at all.

Special efforts are needed right from childhood to inculcate the habit of merging into a team. The ego of individual players is the main hindrance for operating as a team. Those who start winning at early stages with their individual talent feel that they have a right to be egoistic, and this is mistaken for confidence. Sharing the responsibility and also the credit for success of the team is the vital requirement for teamwork.

Leading players in sports get so involved in their own achievements that they start considering their own team members as their rivals. This spells doom for the team performance. This selfish attitude to hog all the chances and credit creates an adversarial feeling in the team. With this feeling, it becomes extremely difficult for anyone to focus properly and express one's skill. Then it becomes impossible to achieve the team goals.

Feeling of compassion and affection for those in the fraternity, acceptance and admiration for their merits should be made a habitual response. Then it is not difficult to perform in any team that you may have to join, even at a short notice.

The key words for inculcating the habit of being a good team member are *sharing* and *caring*. Share the joy of winning, the reward, the credit, the responsibility of facing challenges and sorrow of failures if any. Just as you should not steal the personal belongings of anyone, you should not grab the credit and the reward also. Be generous in your approach and give credit to your partners in any team, wherever it is due. You will have to establish a relation, a very close emotional bond with the members of your team in which you are working. This relation is the result of the habit of caring for the position, thought and comforts of others. Your body language and behaviour should make it clear to your teammates that you care for them.

Personal likes and dislikes are mostly instinctive, and create internal groups, which are very dangerous for the team, for these groups start working against each other and the common goal is lost sight of. Then that team has very poor chances of winning. Whenever there is a clash of goals, the team goals should get priority and individual goals have to be sacrificed. In all decisions, moves and even in thoughts, the team should be regarded as supreme and its interests should be protected.

The tree is an excellent example of teamwork provided to us by nature. The roots, the stem, the branches, the leaves, the flowers and fruits all have specific roles to play. Yet the whole world is attracted to the flowers and fruits. The rest of the tree does not receive so much adoration. But they continue to provide support to the flowers and fruits. The roots dig themselves deep into the earth and the stems and branches carry the food gathered all over the tree and also give it support. The leaves collect energy from the air and serve as lungs. If any of these parts refuse to cooperate because the flowers and fruits get all the credit, survival of the plant itself will be a major problem. Similarly, in the human body, the whole system participates for its well-being, but it is only the right hand that goes ahead for the reward. If the rest of the body allows the feeling of jealousy to take command, no achievement will be possible.

The process of selection, leadership and seniority are factors, which are not under the control of the members of the team. The coach and the manager are supposed to be vital contributors for realizing the goals. They are important members of the team itself. They should act and be treated as such. I pity the selectors. For any team selected, they are bound to displease a number of others who are not included. They have to depend on the past performances for the process of selection and for any failure on part of those selected, they are criticized. Then those selected keep worrying about their continuation in the team for future events. Those not selected have to participate at lower levels, and they keep sulking that they were overlooked. All these negative attitudes affect their performance. The commitment of all sportsmen should be to perform at their best in every match they play. Even at the highest level of competition, it is essential that they focus on the expression of their skills rather than on thoughts about what would happen in the future. Same is true about those who are dropped from the team, and have to perform at lower levels. Unless they excel at that level, they will be justifying the action of the selectors in excluding them from the team.

Since no one has the final say in the selection of the team in which they have to play, one must learn to adjust with the teammates just as one has to adjust to the playing conditions in any match. Adjustment of the techniques and strategies to the conditions prevailing is a vital quality of all the champions. Most challenging condition is merging into the team you have to be a part of. Responses can keep changing and become unpredictable in the case of human beings. There can be misunderstandings, if not intentional mischief, and relations may get sour. Instinctive likes and dislikes have to be kept aside, points of agreement have to be sought out and kept in focus so that the disagreement over some issues does not get prominence.

The common goals should never be neglected and individual goals should never get precedence over them. Then keeping a look out for the excellence of teammates and expressing appreciation over it helps in establishing a bond. If any of the players commits a mistake, other team-mates should forgive him immediately and show it in their body language and utterances. If the player is condemned verbally and by gestures, it will affect his mood and focus. Then he is likely to commit costlier mistakes. The player should also be determined to focus more on the expression of his skill for the rest of the game, and stop fretting over the past mistakes as quickly as possible.

In every team there is a mixture of different kinds of human beings. Some are good mixers; some are serious and quiet, while some are frivolous. The general tendency is to select a scapegoat and make him the butt end of verbal and practical jokes. This affects his performance and the team efforts also. Seniority and brilliance are two factors, which tend to create problems in team feeling. Sometimes senior players do not get due respect and their expectations also might be exaggerated. Then brilliance and form do not depend on seniority, and feelings of rivalry start developing. All the players should be very careful in establishing close bonds and a sense of belonging in the team. Effort should be made to change the team into one cohesive family and work towards the goals. First-name familiarity and encouraging verbal exchanges during the recovery phases of the game go a long way to achieve this result.

Whatever be the differences amongst the team members, they should be shelved or sunk before the beginning of the match. Team leadership has the main responsibility to ensure that all members of the team blend into a cohesive group. The captain should realize that he is a player and part of the team first, and has been given the additional responsibility of making decisions. The decisions to be taken have to be in the interest of the team and not to project himself or any individual. It is the captain who has to bring the focus on the team goals again and again.

The captain should be accessible and open for suggestions. Regular team meetings for planning and explaining strategies should be held. The coach, captain, vice captain, manager and all the team members must attend these meetings. They should not only be meeting for briefings, but everyone must feel free to contribute and suggest in such meetings. The roles and goals should be defined in very clear terms and the players must know the strategy to be followed in the match, in advance. The leadership is supposed to surprise the opponents by sudden shifts in the strategy.

The captain has the responsibility of decisions and the performance of the whole team. He tends to forget that he has to perform as a player also. Once the decision in the captain's role is made, he has to become the player in the active phase of the game. He must inculcate the habit of making this role-shift very effective and total. There have been great captains who have led their teams to victory and made very significant contributions as players also. They should be the role models for those who want to make a mark as a captain.

Parades, drill, exercising together, group activities other than the sport itself are of great use for building up the team spirit. Establishing personal and family-like relations amongst the team members by celebrating birthdays and memorable days and anniversaries together is also useful. Group singing, praying and meditating together also help in bonding with the teammates. To develop team feeling, practising Jyoti Trataka, a form of meditation, together, is of great help. When the teams are entering the ground to play matches, it is best to forget the differences. Some gestures like dipping hands in water, touching a pole or a tree as one enters the field with the thought that all differences of opinion are being washed off or handed over to the pole or the tree, are useful in building and maintaining the team spirit during a match. Touch indicates acceptance. Shaking hands, patting on the back, 'high fives' and huddling together for celebrating successful moments of joy are quite useful in cultivating the sense of belonging, which is so vital for team performance.

Sincere efforts to develop the qualities of being a good team member prove to be rewarding not only in sports, but also in all walks of life. Then why not include those in your daily schedules?

ACTION POINTS

- Players should be willing to merge and blend their individual excellence into group effort and work for a common goal.

- Sharing the responsibility and also the credit for success of the team is the vital requirement for teamwork.

- The key words for inculcating the habit of being a good team member are 'sharing' and 'caring'.

- The tree and the human body are excellent examples of teamwork.

- Common goals should never be neglected and individual goals should never get precedence over them.

- Seniority and brilliance are two factors, which tend to create problems in team feelings.

- It is the captain who has to bring the focus on the team goals again and again.

- Once the decision in the captain's role is made, he has to become the player in the active phase of the game.

- Sincere efforts to develop the qualities of being a good team member prove to be rewarding not only in sports, but also in all walks of life.

14

Stress, Anxiety and Motivation

Remember the joy you felt when you first learnt swimming? (If you have not learnt swimming, you have really missed something in your life!) What a great time we had in our childhood in playing with water, the strange, yielding medium. Then someone introduced me to competitive swimming. I found myself just swimming up and down the length of the pool. It did not take me long to get thoroughly bored and I started dodging the practice sessions.

My swimming coach, Abdul Majid, was actually an illiterate person in the sense that he did not know how to read and write. But his knack for learning skills and teaching others was simply fantastic. I have rarely come across persons of his calibre in any field. He sensed my feeling of boredom. He made me watch *Tarzan* and a film showing the Commonwealth Games held at Vancouver, Canada. I felt inspired by the easy propulsion style of Johnny Weismuller, who was one of the best Tarzans on screen, and the then world champion butterfly stroke swimmer, Georgi Tumpek.

Thereafter, my training laps in the swimming pool never bored me. They became experiments in the skill of attaining speed using the resistance offered by the element of water. I also got the taste of joy of winning in competitions. No doubt, I started suffering from the anxiety and stress that arose from the concepts of victory and loss. But I could also learn to overcome these feelings and perform well, in spite of them.

Even the greatest achievers in the world have suffered from excessive stress and anxiety. These traits are quite natural to human beings. You are caught between two prongs of a very well-known past and a totally uncertain future. You hope to meet the challenges in the future with the experience that you have gathered in the past. In competition, you realize very soon that the factors in challenges that you have to face are so numerous that it is impossible to learn how to deal with them with the skills your past experiences have given you. They are useful without any doubt but not adequate at all.

In addition to this, the failures that have occurred in the unforgettable past keep nagging you. They raise doubts about your capability to face the challenge and the possibility of failure starts looming large. This makes you anxious about the outcome of future events and this anxiety, in turn, builds up stress in your mind. It eats up all your energies very fast and makes you weak, affecting your decision making.

What a pleasure it would be to remain free from all stress and tensions! But this will never happen. You must bear in mind that all stress is not bad. It is also useful for achievement. Anxiety and stress are indicators of your deep interest in what you are doing. Attending to routine chores very seldom gives you stress. Once the task becomes a routine one, your inner power gets a message that it can be handled without paying much attention to details. Then the power of focus gets diverted elsewhere.

The deep interest and the feeling of challenge have to be nursed and developed carefully. Some anxiety of the outcome will remain, but you can easily take care of it. Real problem starts when this feeling gets converted into a nagging worry. Then all the eagerness and curiosity about the future get converted into the emotion of fear and the problem becomes more complicated. Faith and commitment to your goals give you the strength to keep stress and anxiety at a manageable level. Then the confidence of facing the challenge successfully does not desert you.

According to the science of yoga, afflictions, which lead to stress and misery should be found out by proper analysis, as early as possible. If the cause is located early, it can be removed very easily. But if the cause takes root and becomes a habit, it can be removed by exercising the choice of focus and by meditating on the object or events selected for focus.

Ignorance, wrong notions about one's own self, attachment to sensual pleasures and detesting unpleasant experiences are at the root of all stress and misery. When you start giving top priority to creature comforts, fall in love with your body, get frightened at the very thought of injury or death, then you tend to forget that the body and all the inner faculties are just the instruments for achieving your goals. Then the various roles that you have to play in life claim priority over what you are actually doing. You must make a firm resolve to follow the schedules you have chalked for achieving excellence. Take charge of your ability to focus and use it whenever you are learning anything or facing a challenge. Learn from the experiences of other achievers as to how they have faced adversities and steered the course away from distractions. Never spare yourself and make the best effort possible to excel.

Remaining in the present and focusing on what you are actually doing is an excellent method for handling excessive stress and anxiety. Soham chant with breathing works very well for remaining focused and reducing stress. Relaxation in the recovery phases of a match by doing Nyasa or consciously relaxing a part of the body also helps a lot.

If you are anxious about something happening outside the sports field, a very good technique to shelve the issue has been mentioned by John Shyer and Christopher Connolly in their book *Sporting Body Sporting Mind*. It is a visualization technique. You relax and visualize that you are writing down the details of the problem which is likely to claim your attention. Mentally, see yourself writing at length about the distraction on a blank sheet of paper and after completing the writing, see yourself folding the sheet of paper and keeping it in a box or a shelf behind you. Then commit yourself to get back to the problem and attend to it after the match or practice session is over. Make it a point to go back to the shelf in your visualization session after the match, fetch the paper and really attend to the problem so that the part of your mind which was getting attracted to the distraction, will feel convinced that you have kept your promise.

We found that the technique works very well and in some cases a modification was introduced. Instead of keeping the paper in the shelf or the box after folding it, visualize that you are handing over the paper to a well-wisher, whom you inform that you have to attend to the problem mentioned in the sheet, after the match or the session is over. The introduction of another person as a well-wisher in the scheme of things helped some of the players better than the concept of keeping it in a box. You may experiment with both the concepts and decide which of them suits you better.

For being successful in the field of sports you will have to make several sacrifices, make a lot of efforts, and face adverse conditions a number of times. Against this background, if the achievement does not get any recognition, you get dropped from the team or have to keep struggling at the same level for a long time, you may start feeling frustrated. You may find it very difficult to get motivated to continue. Other acute problems in inter-personal relations like rejection in love and loss of a dear one may also drain away your motivation to play and perform at your best. Prospects of a future career, besides playing, may become the cause of insecurity and a strong demotivating factor.

Playing becomes an excellent diversion for troubles in other walks of life. This is where one should draw inspiration from the examples of great personalities in sports who have faced tough times all along and still managed to reach the top. It is one's commitment and resolve to excel in the sport that can see oneself through these problems. Keep reinforcing this commitment by a convincing self-talk. Do not go by what others say, but go by your feelings and you will find that you remain motivated. Love not only your sport, but love the challenges also. Then you are sure to excel.

ACTION POINTS

- Anxiety and stress are indicators of your deep interest in what you are doing.
- According to the science of yoga, afflictions which lead to stress and misery should be found out by proper analysis as early as possible.
- Remaining in the present and focusing on what you are actually doing is an excellent method for handling excessive stress and anxiety.
- For being successful in the field of sports, you will have to make several sacrifices, make lots of efforts and will have to face adverse conditions a number of times.
- Take charge of your ability to focus and use it whenever you are learning anything or facing a challenge.
- Love not only your sport, but also the challenges. Then you are sure to excel.

15

Competition Season

I was playing a snooker match. Two tables were accommodated in the corner of a huge hall. The rest of the hall was being used for the annual badminton tournament of the club. Only a cloth curtain separated the snooker and badminton areas. My match was in the decider frame. As luck would have it, I was on the table with an extremely favourable position and I was about to finish the cue action for a pot. Suddenly I was startled with a sudden explosion of applause from behind the curtain and my cue brushed the ball before I could stop the action. I was penalized four points and I lost not only my turn at the table, but also the match, for the opponent gleefully cleared the table. I knew that the badminton match was going on in the same hall and should have been ready for a sudden disturbance by spectator applause. There was a noticeable lull in the noise coming from across the curtain, but in the excitement of being offered the match on a platter because of the favourable position, I forgot the likelihood of disturbance, and paid the price.

In a match, there can be a number of such distractions. There may be a sudden movement or a loud noise or a commotion amongst the spectators because of the arrival of some well-known figure. Whenever there are several matches or competitions going on at the same venue, you will have to have a sharper focus and be prepared to take a break or make necessary allowance for such occurrences.

There is a concept of attaining the 'peak' form during the major competition season. You will have to decide in advance, which are the most important competitions for you in the forthcoming season. You should then plan your physical and mental preparation in such a manner as to make your best form coincide with the top competition. If you are preparing for the Olympics to be held in the month of August, then your peak form should not be reached in July or September. Peaking early or late can spell disaster.

You will also have to plan your training schedules properly. There is a tendency to take heavy overload as the major competition season approaches. This should be avoided. Actually, the energy reserves should be created during the off-season and preserved during the period approaching the competition season.

The same rule applies to the improvement of technique and major changes in it. Sometimes the players experience loss of form on the eve of or during the tournament season. Then the technique becomes suspect and tips are sought from experts to improve the skill itself.

A very careful analysis of the loss of form is necessary. In the majority of cases, it is due to pressures building up from other roles in life and loss of focus due to too much attachment to result. In such cases, sincere efforts to improve the quality of focus yield excellent results in a very short time span.

You should avoid making any major changes to your technique, as far as possible, unless you have sufficient time to work on them. You have built up the responses by long-time practice of the old technique. The habit of producing those responses has to be changed, if you are going to adopt a new technique. It is much better to stick to your earlier system and make efforts to build a sharper focus and confidence, at least till the peak season is over.

Then you can start all over again for the next season with the new technique.

This holds good for equipment also. It takes time for your system to get used to the equipment for your sport. Great players may endorse and recommend specific technique or equipment. You must always bear in mind that they are champions because of the ceaseless efforts they have put in for perfecting the technique, and the ability to adjust to the equipment, environment and playing conditions. So, unless there is an emergency, do not change your equipment or the technique, just before or during the peak season.

As the competition season approaches, the anxiety level goes up and it is very difficult to remember the sequence of things to be done and the list of articles to be taken along with you to the venue of the competitions. You should prepare a checklist of all these things in your diary and go through it sufficiently in advance, so that you reach the venue of the competition, well-prepared.

You should also ensure that you reach the venue well ahead of the time scheduled. If the competition is at some place other than your hometown, make sure you know the address well and how to reach there.

One of my colleagues had a very embarrassing experience. We had gone for a shooting competition and he missed his event, as he could not locate the place. By the time he reached there, his event was over. Our coach quipped, 'You have created a new record. Some shooters fire washout shots by missing the target. You have managed to miss the shooting range itself!'

Competitions involve a lot of travel and you must be able to perform at your best at every place and time irrespective of the conditions prevailing there.

You must ensure that you get proper food and rest. Before going to the place find out the food habits of the people, their language and customs. Unwittingly, you may anger someone and there may be a controversy that might distract you during the competitions. Get into the habit of eating for your stomach and not for your palate. The coach, manager and parents, if any of them are accompanying the athlete, should make efforts to ensure that nourishing food (as far as possible with an agreeable taste) is available.

Because of the amount of travel required to be done, the player has to sacrifice some of the practice sessions. At the venue, there may not be adequate facility to train. Weather may not permit your outdoor fitness schedules. You may find that there is quite a bit of time on your hands to spend. Then you do not know what to do. Getting bored or allowing adversarial feelings like anger, frustration, annoyance, irritation, etc., to develop, will spoil your mood and form.

You get restless thinking that you must put in specific amount of practice every day, or it will be very difficult to play at your best. This is a very wrong notion. If you have acquired a skill by regular practice, it does not desert you just because you have missed a few practice sessions.

Whenever you have to spend time in travelling or waiting for your turn, spend it either in visualization or in some other activity of your interest like reading or listening to music. Whenever possible you should watch the matches being played by others. This gives you a good idea about their style and some tips about the skill and strategy, which might prove useful to you.

You must get into the habit of reaching well in time for your match. Once the match is announced, you should get ready mentally and physically. Build up the mood, focus on the responses, and let your skill flow right from the word 'go'. You should do some light cardiovascular exercises, stretching and dry run of all the movements you have to do during the match as a part of warming up for the match. Before that, you should have the mental warm up in which you familiarize yourself with the signals and situation at the venue, plan your strategy and visualize the major transition points being handled. Then visualize your performance at the start, midway and at the finish. Then you slide into the physical warm up.

Use the recovery phase for defocusing, building confidence through self-talk, relaxation, planning strategy, replenishing energy through deep breathing. In the active phase, shift the focus from breathing to the technique. Involve yourself fully with the action. Maintain the same depth of focus for a little while even after the match or the competition is over. Keep reminding yourself that the match gets over only when you go and shake hands with the opponent.

Learning to control your temper in the match season is of vital importance. Unless you do that, the anxiety you are feeling for the result of your efforts may result in wrong responses in your dealing with others and surprise situations. You have to be extremely careful in your behaviour throughout the competition season to ensure that you do not land into unnecessary troubles, which may distract you from your goals. You will have to celebrate all your successes and those of your friends and the teammates. But you should take care that these do not spoil your training schedules.

Over and above all, be extremely careful about your health. Eat well, practise well, rest well and play well. If you fall ill or injure yourself, you may lose all your chances of winning and all your efforts throughout the year may go waste. Why allow that?

ACTION POINTS

- You need to plan your schedules properly.
- As far as possible, you should avoid making major changes in your technique unless you have sufficient time to work on them.

- Competitions involve a lot of travel and you must be able to perform at your best at every place and time irrespective of the conditions prevailing there.

- Get into the habit of eating for your stomach and not for your palate.

- Keep reminding yourself that the match gets over only when you go and shake hands with the opponent.

- Eat well, practise well, rest well and play well.

PART II

TECHNIQUES FOR IMPROVEMENT IN SKILLS AND PERFORMANCE

16

Building of Self-talk

DIARY OF EXCELLENCE

Self-talk is exercising control over your verbal thoughts. If this emanates from the teachings of masters or your own experience and faith, it becomes more powerful and directs your moods, emotions and actions properly. Then the flow of skills becomes natural and easy; the choice of responses, their execution and overall performance improve considerably. It is also of great help in focusing, refocusing, maintaining confidence level, handling adversities and distractions.

Maintaining a diary of excellence is of great help for verbalizing the best that you have done. Whenever you have done something really well or you have come across thoughts, which you feel will bring about improvement in your technique or performance, jot them down in the diary of excellence. These thoughts may come to you from experts in whom you have faith, or from your own contemplation.

It is advisable to write the diary of excellence on loose sheets of paper and keep them in a file. Then it becomes easy for you to make changes or modifications as and when required by just changing the relevant sheets.

Reinforce the Best in the Diary

This diary should be divided into three parts. The first part should have pages dealing with the past. Describe every past experience of the joy of good performance or achievement in the first part. It is an excellent means to build up your self-image, which is your own impression about yourself. We can call it bio-data training. If you are asked to give your bio-data to anyone, you will only describe your achievements and success, for you want to impress that person. Here, the effort is to impress your own self. As you verbalize the best of your past, it gets visualized and, later on, whenever you read it again, the memory of those experiences is activated and they get visualized. Then the inner power gets a message that you want such experiences to be repeated. Negative memories get checked and positive memories replace them. Then these memories give rise to positive thoughts.

In the second part, you should keep blank loose sheets. You are practising regularly and also playing matches. You keep getting tips from your coach and from other experts whom you consult on various aspects of your skill and performance. You also watch other brilliant players, including your role models, perform. Then you may come across some good tips while reading about your sport. Whenever you are happy with a particular experience or performance or if some specific thought attracts you, feel qualified to write the diary of excellence on that day.

If you are happy with a particular practice session, a match, your fightback, any specific part of the performance like a particular shot, depth of focus, easy flow of skill, etc., describe those in this second part of your diary. As you are trying to find correct words for describing that experience, the thought processes in your mind get visualized. They etch the experience clearly in your memory. The repeated visualization taking place, converts the verbal thoughts into non-verbal experience and your muscle memory gets reinforced with correct responses while writing. The same thing happens every time you read that matter subsequently.

By describing the experiences, you strengthen your *sankalpa* or the verbal expression of your will power. The focused perception of all the relevant signals, selection of the proper responses and the actual response should also be described. Then describe the joy you felt while going through the experience. If you have earned praise from anyone else or won a specific reward, make a mention of that also.

Besides expertise in the skill required for your game, other skills like communication, establishing relations, eliciting proper response from others, giving tips to your colleagues, sharing knowledge and joy, etc. are also important for the development of your personality. Whenever you feel happy about your performance in these aspects, make it a point to describe those experiences in your diary. As you go on filling the loose sheets in the second part, they get added to the first part describing the past brilliance.

In the third part, write about your goals. State the ultimate goals of your career in unambiguous terms. Then spell out the phases and short-term goals also, quite clearly. Write about your commitment to these goals, the efforts you have planned and the sacrifices you are willing to make. As you write the third part, the direction in which you want to shape the future gets defined. Describe in details what you want to achieve, how you are going to do that and why. Write about the joy you will feel, when you achieve your goals. Keep reading this third part as often as possible and add to it whatever positive thoughts that may strike you. Reading this part will help you in visualizing your skill and performance while meeting future challenges.

You will realize that the diary consists of experiences of excellence achieved in the past and the goals to be achieved in future. Whenever you describe anything that has given you real satisfaction, it adds to your bio-data of achievements in the past. The diary of excellence helps you in keeping your focus on the best in the past, present and future. It builds up a positive self-image and gives you the confidence required for facing tough challenges in the sport chosen or any other field, for that matter.

Initially, try and describe the experiences in details. Later on, you develop the skill to be brief and to the point. Since you describe the thought processes and the resultant action, it gives you an excellent base for a positive self-talk to keep your focus, mood and confidence at the required level. Then you can fight negative thoughts, adversities and stay away from distractions more effectively. You automatically cultivate the habit of winning.

P. Gopichand, the badminton star, has made the best use of the diary of excellence. When he met me in Prakash Padukone Academy at Bangalore in 1998, I found that his talents and sincere efforts were clouded by the focus on negative experiences and thoughts. He had not won the national title till then and the national championships were just three weeks away. Besides the exercises for improving focus, I suggested that he use the technique of positive verbalization through the diary of excellence. Three weeks later, when we met again at the venue of the national championships, I was impressed by the efforts made by him when I saw his diary. The focus had been shifted to positive thoughts and experiences. I realized that he would be unbeatable if he continued to think in this line and I told him so. He proved it by winning the national title without dropping a single game in the whole tournament and went on to win the All England title also.

In the diary of excellence, there is no place for negative statements. If flaws have been noticed, mention what you are doing to remove those and how you will perform when you have succeeded in doing so. Writing the diary of excellence regularly will keep your focus on positive experiences and thoughts. Whenever you find the time, glance through a few pages of the diary. You will be able to find out the cue words or phrases for positivizing the thought processes, whenever you feel depressed due to negative thoughts. You will find the convincing arguments against any doubts that may arise in your mind about your capacity to deal with the challenge that you are to face. You will have a strong, positive self-image and will never be wanting in confidence.

DIARY OF EXCELLENCE

Write the diary of excellence on loose sheets of paper and keep them in a file. It will be useful for building up a convincing self-talk.

This diary should have three parts:

- The first part should deal with the past. In this part, describe whatever you have done best in the past.

- In the second part, you should keep blank loose sheets. You are practising regularly and also playing matches. Whenever you are happy with a particular experience, performance or when some specific thought attracts you, feel qualified to write the diary of excellence on that day.

- In the third part, write about your goals. State the ultimate goals of your career in unambiguous terms. Then spell out the phases and short term goals also quite clearly. Write about your commitment to these goals, the efforts you have planned and the sacrifices you are willing to make. As you write the third part, the direction in which you want to shape the future gets defined.

JAPA: THE CHANTING OF MANTRAS

Mantras are thoughts expressed through words, phrases or sentences. Sometimes, only a single syllable pronunciation like 'Om' or a catchword or phrase is used as a mantra. (The chanting of mantras is one of the best methods of controlling thought processes and improving concentration.) As mentioned earlier, all actions originate from thoughts and our line of thinking also governs our moods and attitudes. Unless we make efforts and take control over the thoughts, we fall into the damaging habit of being dragged along aimlessly by uncontrolled thoughts. Then concentration becomes very difficult.

Words used for mantras have to be those in which you have faith. These have to be obtained from experts in whom we have faith or to be found out by verbalization of our own experiences. The thought processes, which have been useful in focusing, refocusing, building up courage and confidence, resisting distractions or facing adversities can also be used for developing the mantras. According to yoga, the initial expertise in concentration is developed through words and by contemplating on their meanings. Subsequently, we get the power to follow thought processes and our experiences directly. Regular chanting of a mantra reminds us of the thoughts it indicates and the line of thought to be followed. This chant can be effective only if two conditions are fulfilled. You will have to focus on its meaning and ensure that the required mood is created by its repeated utterance. To achieve this effect, you must have full faith in the thought indicated or expressed through the mantra.

The process of controlling your thought processes through mantras is to be used for reinforcing your faith in yourself, your technique, knowledge, skill and the ability to utilize all these. Analysis sessions with your coaches, experts and knowledgeable persons; knowledge acquired through reading books; your own reflection and visualization of past experiences are useful in finding out the catch phrases, cue words or sentences, which can be used as mantras directing your self-talk. Repeated chant of these mantras, then, enable you to control the thought processes while facing challenges.

While writing the diary of excellence or your *sankalpa*, you should minutely go through the experience of brilliant performances in the past. If you contemplate on your mental frame during such experiences, you will learn what thoughts were fleeting through your mind when the events and your responses were unfolding themselves. Verbalize these thoughts, especially when you have fought back from a losing position; or whenever doubts had taken charge of your mind and you had managed to quell them. Then you will be in a position to find the words to be used as mantras for starting these thought processes again.

Mantras or the thoughts developed from your own experience can also be used very effectively as convincing arguments in favour of your capacity, skill and knowledge. You have to look for and identify these thoughts and then verbalize them carefully. You, then, chant these with full focus on their meaning, whenever doubts have the upper hand and your faith in yourself or the self-image gets damaged. What has worked for you earlier is easily acceptable to your system and can work very well again. While formulating these mantras, make sure that you are able to convince yourself by dwelling on these thoughts. You can also make extensive use of what you read from the experiences of other achievers and also whatever expert advice that may be available.

The mantras for fighting distractions and adversities are actually reminders of your commitment and the choice of focus. I came across some sportsmen trying to use 'I am going to win' as a mantra to be repeatedly chanted during the recovery phase of the game. But this causes the attention to be focused on the result of the match and actually distracts the mind from what is to be done or from the technique itself. As you enter the active phase, some mantras like 'Focus on the ball' or 'play the shuttle' are more useful as they remind you of what you are supposed to do to remain fully in the present and ensure the even flow of your skill.

The mantras for quelling doubts and reinforcing faith are actually arguments and are often longer than the mantras to be used in the active phase of the game. Sometimes just a catchword or phrase is enough to remind you of what is to be done. Words or phrases like 'faster', 'move', 'calm down', 'smash', 'toss', etc. can be used as mantras, but do not choose them blindly because someone else is suggesting. Find out what works for you and then make a record in your diary and make it a point to use the mantra as self-talk whenever required. If you form a habit of focusing on the thought indicated by the mantra and get into the proper mood by its use, you are supposed to have mastered the mantra. Once you achieve this, you can control your emotions, moods and distractions very effectively and are better equipped to face adverse conditions.

Even in the case of interpersonal relations and building up teamwork, you can find out and use mantras extensively. When the behaviour of your teammate is annoying you and there is the likelihood of developing adversarial feeling, you run the risk of underperforming as it can affect your ability to focus. Keep telling yourself that the person is an invaluable asset to your team and you should not hold such odd occurrences against him. Mantras like, 'I love him', 'I respect him' and 'I forgive him' can convince you of the everlasting need of building a rapport between team members.

Make efforts to find out the mantras that work for you and keep on chanting them focusing on their meaning. This is a very effective method of controlling your self-talk. You will automatically get to perform much better in all times and conditions. Then you would be able to cultivate one of the essential habits for winning.

JAPA: THE CHANTING OF MANTRAS

- Mantras are thoughts expressed through words, phrases or sentences.
- Words used for mantras have to be those in which you have faith.
- This chant can be effective only if two conditions are fulfilled. You need to focus on its meaning and ensure that the required mood is created by its repeated utterance.
- Analysis sessions with your coaches, experts and knowledgeable persons; knowledge acquired through reading books; your own reflection and visualization of the past experiences are useful in finding out the catch phrases, cue words or sentences, which can be used as mantras directing your self-talk.

SANKALPA: PRAYER AND COMMITMENT

We are examining the methods of using the verbal thought processes for building up your focus, confidence and ability to face adversities, and staying away from distractions. Verbal thoughts have to be controlled as they lead to all the actions, correct or otherwise. Whenever you look to the future, two kinds of thoughts occupy your mind. You think of success or of failure in the task you have undertaken. The common tendency is to allow the thoughts of failure occupy your mind and then get involved with them. This is known as *vikalpa* or negative imagination. The thoughts which convince you that you are going to complete the task successfully are known as *sankalpa* or positive imagination. Both the processes form part of imagination as you are looking into the future, the territory of the unknown. Unless you take command of the thought processes, your mind indulges in *vikalpa*, entertaining negative thoughts and the inner power gets a totally wrong message, that you are interested in failing. *Sankalpa* is an exercise in training your mind to remain involved with positive thoughts about the future. It takes care of the habit of indulging in *vikalpa*.

When you study any of the Upanishads, you have to chant a shanti mantra both at the beginning and at the end of the study. The shanti mantra consists of two parts: the first is the commitment to keep your inner faculties calm and focused and the second is a prayer to the deities and the powers that control your surroundings to maintain peace around you so that you can pursue your study properly. These shanti mantras serve the dual purpose of reminding you of the commitment to remain calm and building up the confidence from the powers that are favourable to you.

Like the shanti mantras, Indian scriptures prescribe the utterance of *sankalpa*, or the statement of what you are going to do, why and how you are going to do it, before undertaking any important task. It is a very useful exercise for excellence in sports, for it directs the thought processes effectively towards excellence. It involves preparing a statement, which reminds you of your commitment to excellence and also expresses a wish or a prayer, that the future event takes place as per your plans. Once you have prepared this statement, you should read it as often as possible with a focus on its meaning. Both while preparing this statement and while reading it subsequently, positive visualization takes place as the thoughts get translated into visualization of positive actions. Then the negative thoughts get curbed and you get into a proper mood for the event, and the natural flow of your skills is also ensured.

Take a sheet of paper and write down the date and venue of the match for which you are preparing the *sankalpa* or the statement. Then mention the event and explain why it is important for you to excel and perform at your best, illustrating your drive, urge and interest in the sport you have chosen. Describe the efforts and sacrifices you have made for acquiring the expertise required to win. You have to convince yourself that you have the qualities and the skill to excel in the event you are preparing for. Mention the hard work put into training, the expert guidance that you have taken, how you have developed the skill; the strength and the stamina to emerge victorious. Then describe the challenges that the event or match will make you face. Write about the focus and confidence with which you are going to face these challenges and the commitment to maintain this attitude and the focus required, till the event gets over and for some time more. Describe the joy you are going to experience when you remain in command and perform with perfect focus and poise. Explain how you will respond to the opponent's strategies and sustain the attitude and mood throughout.

In the last part, think that the event is over and looking back, write about the response of others to your excellence, the result you have obtained, and the natural consequences of your brilliance, like going into the next round, or winning the title, getting selected for the higher level of matches, etc.

In short, you will have to project yourself as playing in the manner you want and winning the match or competition. If you feel that you find it difficult to describe the future, imagine you have won the match and then describe it as a flashback. This type of verbalization is also useful as it starts the positive thought processes and the same benefit will accrue in building up the proper attitude and responses.

Then keep this sheet of paper in your diary of excellence and read it as many times as possible every day. This, then, becomes your daily prayer, and try and repeat it as often as possible. Keep the focus on the meaning of the words you have written. Then the mood and attitude start getting built up. The thoughts get visualized automatically and equip you much better to face the challenges the event will put up before you.

It is very important to think about the responses of others because negative thoughts mostly originate from imagining the criticism one may receive from others if one performs below their expectations. It is safer to imagine the response of your well-wishers and describe it in the *sankalpa* statement rather than writing about the response of those who do not like you or have a negative attitude.

SANKALPA: PRAYER AND COMMITMENT

Whenever you visualize the future, two kinds of thoughts occupy your mind. You think of success or of failure in the task you have undertaken.

- The common tendency is to allow the thoughts of failure occupy your mind and then get involved with them. This is known as *vikalpa* or negative imagination.

- The thoughts, which convince you that you are going to complete the task successfully, are known as *sankalpa* or positive imagination.

The process of preparing the *sankalpa* statement itself starts the flow of positive thoughts and their visualization. Reading it as often as possible with involvement and focus serves as the prayer and also as a reminder of your commitments.

ACTION POINTS

- Take a sheet of paper and write down the date and venue of the match for which you are preparing the *sankalpa* or the statement.
- Then mention the event and explain why it is important for you to excel and perform at your best.
- Mention the hard work put into training, the expert guidance that you have taken and how you have developed the skill, the strength and the stamina to emerge victorious.
- Then describe the challenges that the event or match will make you face.
- Explain how you will respond to the opponent's strategies, and sustain the attitude and mood throughout.
- In the last part, think that the event is over and looking back, write about the response of others to your excellence, the result you have obtained, and the natural consequences of your brilliance.
- In short you will have to project yourself as playing in the manner you want and winning the match or competition.
- This, then, becomes your daily prayer. Try and repeat it as often as possible. Keep the focus on the meaning of the words you have written.

17

Visualization:
Improvement of
Self-image

RELIVING THE BEST IN THE PAST

Memory of the past is a special power of human beings. Assisted by the power of expression, the mind has a habit of continuously slipping into the past and reliving the experiences. This habit is dangerous and quite damaging if you allow your mind to have the choice of focus in this regard. It invariably chooses the unwanted, miserable experiences from the past and goes on remembering them in minute details. All these details get visualized and since this happens repeatedly, the inner power gets a wrong message that you are interested in getting these experiences again. It, then, produces the same responses leading to the same mistakes and you start wondering why this is happening. On the face of it, these mistakes appear so silly that you find it difficult to forgive yourself and forget them. Then if you are an established player, there are a number of fans, the press and the coach, friends, and so on to remind you as to how foolish you have been. They will not allow you to forget that one mistake, even if you are trying to do so.

In the process of remembering the mistakes and failures vividly, you tend to forget whatever you have done well in the past. Taking charge of the memory and dwelling on the past brilliance is a very difficult task, because of the natural tendency of your mind to keep the focus on negatives, throughout your life. But it is the most important task and has to take priority over everything else. Once you inculcate the habit of keeping the focus on the best things that have happened in the past you are able to improve your skills and techniques. You also get the confidence of their easy flow in challenging conditions.

The great batting master, Sachin Tendulkar, once described to me the sad experience of getting out on a wonderful batting pitch to an ordinary ball. Almost everyone else on both the sides had scored well and he had got out for no score. I shared his misery as a fan of his and had the same feelings. But, for him it was very risky to remember and unintentionally visualize that experience over and over again. I told him, 'You are really lucky to have chosen a skill which does not allow more mistakes. In games like tennis, you have a chance to make up for the mistakes in the same match or to make fresh mistakes. But as a batsman, you commit one mistake and you are back in the pavilion. This is a sudden death format and you will have to wait till the next chance to bat again. In your case the number of mistakes you have committed is surprisingly small and that is why you are Sachin. For every wrong tackling of the ball, you have innumerable instances of doing it in a perfect manner. Why allow the minority of such incidents to have a major claim on your attention-focus? Why not try and remember the instances when you have tackled similar deliveries in a better manner?'

The basic idea is to convince yourself that you can do a particular thing and do it well under all circumstances. The efforts of writing the diary of excellence, self-talk, and finding out mantras or catch phrases and words have to be done with the same intention. Visualization is a more advanced method than these verbal exercises. For it is possible to visualize only if you have faith. Since we are talking of your own experience, why should you not believe it? Actually it is just a matter of shifting the focus to the positive experiences of your past. You should not allow any of those experiences to be forgotten.

You do not have to be Sachin Tendulkar to do this. Even if your correct actions are in a miserable minority, you will have to give them strength by keeping focus on them, verbalizing them in your diary and visualizing them repeatedly. Then the proper responses will start appearing more frequently and your skill and performance will improve. Catching yourself doing things right is the key for doing this. Be on the look out for excellence in your performance. Do not allow yourself to forget it. At the earliest opportunity, verbalize it in your diary and visualize it again and again. It is advisable to do this regularly. Whatever best you have done during the day, mention it in your diary and visualize it in minute details as vividly as possible.

Visualizing an object clearly is in itself a difficult thing. Then in sports, there is something or the other happening continuously. The whole chain of events is important for you and should be clearly etched in your memory. Your skill involves the successful handling of several transition points. Each transition point is an event and you should reinforce in your memory all such events in which you have handled the transition points well. When you are trying to learn a particular part of the skill, observe your role model executing that part of the skill, then visualize it in your memory. Then replace the role model by your own self and experience the event, especially the handling of the transition points.

As a player, you will realize that the precise handling of the transition points requires a chain of preparatory actions. The transition point triggers off the follow-through action. But all this is preceded by the thought processes going on in the player's mind. It is laid down in yoga that if you concentrate fully on the actions of a person, you will be able to read what is going on in his mind. If you are watching a champion in action, your focus should be so sharp that you are able to know the thought processes going on in his mind. Then the secret of his being a champion is revealed to you.

Those who are serious about performance in sports should make it a point to watch the champions or the role models in action. Now the facility of recording matches and practice sessions on video CDs is available. It should be used extensively to assist visualization of the champion's style and also your own best performances.

Dropping the habit of indulging in the thoughts of the past failures and cultivating the habit of reinforcing excellence by remembering or visualizing a positive experience and reinforcing it is known as purification of memory in yoga. Whenever you have excelled and have enjoyed the natural flow of your skills, it is like a spiritual experience. Reliving the best spiritual experiences involves a technique known as Manas Puja. It teaches you to remember and visualize a spiritual experience like visiting a holy place, meditating on the image of the deity you may be worshipping or the experience of a personal meeting with your guru. While doing this exercise, all the verbal assistance required should be taken in the beginning. As you become used to remembering the minute details of the experience, you start visualizing the event clearly and the verbal support is not needed.

For a player, experiencing the flow of skill in a brilliant performance is just like a spiritual experience. The diary of excellence will provide all the self-talk needed for the verbal support. As you advance in the skill of meditating on the actual event through visualization, the need for verbal support starts reducing and finally vanishes. Your mind has a habit of responding to cues. In your brilliance and flow of skill, the responses to the cues coming from the surroundings at the venue also have a role to play. Both physical and mental warm-up for the event are also important as they give rise to the thought processes producing the proper responses required for the game. Whenever you have experienced excellence, relive that event at the earliest opportunity. Try and remember as many details as possible about that experience and use them during the visualization sessions. Do not fight shy of using words to build up the memory till you develop the skill of visualization without having to depend on verbal thoughts.

If you are a religious person, you can use your visits to the temple, church, mosque or whatever religious place you might be frequently visiting for building up the visualization capacity. If you are not of the religious bent of mind, try and remember the visit to any place which has given you the feeling of joy. Being aware of nature's beauty and infinity are experiences which are close to spiritual experiences and that is why they are so much sought after. A visit to any picturesque place can also be remembered and visualized for practising the purification of memory skills. But you should remember that there is a major difference in remembering a sports event and a spiritual experience. It is your active participation in the event that you have to reinforce in the memory. You are responding to the cues coming forth in the natural flow of the skill and that is the most important part of the event you have to meditate upon. Once you purify your memory of the past and become adept in the skill of visualizing the past events, you can tackle the other more difficult part of visualization skill, that is, the anticipation of future events.

RELIVING THE BEST IN THE PAST

- The basic idea is to convince yourself that you can do a particular thing and do it well under all circumstances.
- Whenever you have excelled and have enjoyed the natural flow of your skills, it is like a spiritual experience. Reliving the best spiritual experiences involves a technique known as Manas Puja.
- Actually, it is just a matter of shifting the focus to the positive experiences in your past. You should not allow any of those experiences to be forgotten.
- Catching yourself doing things right and reliving the experience is the key for doing this.

VISUALIZING THE FUTURE

Visualizing the future is the most difficult type of visualization but all the efforts to master this skill are very rewarding, for all preparations have to be for matches to be played in the future. The past is very well known while the future is always totally unknown. Remembering and visualizing the past is comparatively an easy skill as the whole of it is stored in your memory. You just have to decide which of the events to focus on. Just like the most common habit of dwelling only on the past miseries and failures, most human beings habitually anticipate only failures and miseries whenever they think of the future. This is known as *vikalpa* or wrong imagination. The opposite of this is the *sankalpa* or the correct imagination of the future, which involves imagining things happening in the manner in which you want them to happen.

Your skill as a player comes from your muscle memory, which reproduces all the correct responses you have brought about. You must bear in mind that the skill comes out and expresses itself as a response to the signals coming at the venue where you are supposed to perform. It is easy to play well on the home ground because the signals are mostly familiar and you feel quite comfortable. But, even while performing at unknown venues, there will be several signals with which it will be easy to familiarize. You should make use of this phenomenon. Wherever you are playing, the size and shape of the court, ground, dimensions, etc., will be the same. In addition, the equipment you are going to use will also be the same and will give you familiar signals.

In visualizing the performance, the signals that you are likely to get at the venue should be pictured. Then observe yourself bringing out your best responses on that background, adopt the role of the performer and get the feel of your responses. Whenever you are expected to perform at a strange venue, spend some time studying the situation and familiarizing yourself with the signals there. Then in your visualization sessions, see yourself performing well on the background of that venue.

In visualizing future matches, your opponents are amongst the signals at the venue. They should be included in the visualization scheme, but the main focus should be on your responses, your technique and the manner in which you handle the transition points. All actions are backed by three powers within you. It is the will power that strengthens your resolve; the power to know and observe keeps you focused on what is happening, and finally, the power to act helps you take correct decisions and implement them. All these powers are used in perfect sequence and coordination, when you are playing in your best form. Then the transition points are handled correctly in perfect rhythm and flow. In visualizing the past, you reinforce all these points in your memory and by visualizing a similar flow of skill at the future venue, you establish a connection between the signals there and your best responses.

Your practice sessions and matches are mostly different because a lot of additional and mostly unfamiliar signals are added, when you are playing a match. The referee and the officials who judge your moves and monitor the following of rules are a major addition. Then the presence of spectators is another prominent factor in a match, which is mostly missing in a practice session. Their presence, the noise of applause or otherwise, and importance of the outcome of the match to you keep on bringing signals, which you are not used to. Just as you are picking up signals from the things happening through your senses, your mind keeps bringing up signals from the past, future, or sometimes totally imaginary and irrelevant to the skill required to win. They may be very trivial, unconnected to your skill or very important to you as a player but not related to what is actually happening. For instance, the end result of the match or the score may be relevant to you as a player, but it is not directly connected with what is actually happening at that precise moment. It can become a major distraction if you allow your mind to get involved with these thoughts. Your mind starts responding to all those signals on its own and you lose focus. In sports, the signals that you have to respond to are in the present and are very much real, while your mind might select imaginary signals from the past, present or future and start responding to them.

If you allow the focus to be shifted to these signals, you are courting disaster. Since they are not relevant to your expression of skill, which alone can win you the match, your will power gets weakened and then the powers of knowledge and response or action also deteriorate. Your observation is not sharp enough and the capacity of selecting and executing the response also gets affected adversely.

Exercising visualization of the match in advance takes care of this problem. In finalizing your visualization schedules, you must take into account all these factors, like the venue, the referee, the officials, the spectators and your likely opponents also. You can familiarize yourself with all these signals and condition your choice of focus and responses. This habit will improve the chances of your winning considerably.

Just as the regular physical practice builds up the ability of responding correctly to the signals, visualization of future events assist in ensuring proper flow of these responses. It is essential to visualize a sharp focus, perfect poise and easy flow of the skill in future events. It is one of the best exercises for developing confidence and appropriate self-image.

Visualization comes very naturally to the leading achievers in sports. They can very easily visualize the future events. As I have mentioned earlier, visualization is a technique of meditation. Some find it very difficult to visualize clearly. They do not have to be disheartened, for this skill can be learned. You should not try to hurry with these processes. Self-talk, visualizing the past and future are all efforts to build up your faith in your own self. You can master them with regular practice and the benefits will be immense. As your faith builds up, go to the higher stage.

There is a simple daily exercise we use for the initiates in visualization skills. I am providing you here with the commentary for the exercise. You may record it in your own voice or in the voice of a well-wisher or the coach. Then, try and follow the instructions by making an attempt to bring the images before your mind's eye.

Initially if the images are not appearing, do not worry. Try and focus on the words and their meaning. Your mind then starts visualizing, though you may not be aware of the images, for quite some time. The coordination between the mind and *wani*, the power of communication, develops gradually. Then the inner power gets a clear message as to what you want to happen. It produces the desired responses automatically, once you get into that situation and pick up the signals chosen.

VISUALIZING THE FUTURE

- Sit on a straight-backed chair and keep your spine straight.
- Surrender to the force of gravity and relax your whole body. Feel the weight of your body on the chair and the feet resting on the ground.
- Focus on your breathing and include the nerve centre at the top of your head in focus. Visualize it sending messages of total relaxation all over your body. Feel the tensions and fatigue in your system disappearing.
- Remember whatever you have done best in the recent past, today, yesterday, day before that, and so on. You can go right up to three weeks in the past.
- Select one of these events and visualize it in minute details. Go to that venue mentally, identify and observe the persons who were there.
- Visualize your focus and poise in the skill flow. Picture how you were focusing only on the relevant signals and how your skill was flowing naturally.
- Feel the joy of achievement you felt. Visualize the response that you got from others, especially your friends and well-wishers.
- Come to the present by focusing on your breathing again. Do deep belly-breathing for one or two minutes.
- Visualize yourself at the venue of your next match or practice session.
- Identify all the signals there and get familiarized with them.
- Visualize yourself warming up, both physically and mentally.
- Visualize the commencement of the match or practice session.
- Observe yourself performing at your best with the same focus and poise as you had in the past best event.
- Visualize yourself completing the event to your satisfaction, and remain in the same focus and mood for some more time.
- Visualize the natural consequences of your excellence—like winning the match, being praised and patted on the back by your coach or a well-wisher.

- Visualize someone presenting you with a beautiful bouquet of flowers. Enjoy the soft touch, the fragrance and the beauty of the flowers enhanced by the lovely arrangement.

- Focus on your breathing again. Do deep belly-breathing for a few breaths, open your eyes slowly and go into a full-body stretch.

CIRCLE OF EXCELLENCE

This is one of the best packages of visualization I have come across. Over 15–20 years ago, I was attending a workshop on sports psychology, when one practising psychologist told us about the circle of excellence. I was fascinated as it was to be used for future events, and it took care of a number of factors required for keeping one's mental balance while facing a challenge.

I started practising it in right earnest. Within a few days, I got a chance to experiment it in a match. It was a billiards league match and I surprised myself and my team by beating a player much better than me and playing in good form. He had beaten me with a comfortable margin in our two previous meetings and was expected to beat me by 100 points in a 200 up game. Instead, I could beat him on 130! Expected to lose 100 points, I had taken 70 points from him!

Subsequently, a lot of players training with me used this technique with excellent results. We went on making modifications as and when required. But the basic technique itself was so good that very little modification was needed. I shall state here the commentary which we use and provide you with my comments on each of the steps. As mentioned earlier, if you are finding it difficult to actually visualize the steps, use the commentary as a self-talk, keeping the focus on the meaning of the words you say to yourself. As you keep practising, visualization skills will develop and you will keep on getting wonderful results.

The technique is not difficult to master and once you get used to it, you can practise it while travelling or waiting for somebody or something like your match, your turn for the practice session, the train or a plane.

- Sit comfortably and focus on your breathing. Include the nerve centre at the top of your head and visualize that nerve centre sending messages of total relaxation all over your body. Feel the tensions and fatigue in your system disappearing.

  Comments: Total relaxation is a precondition for all visualization exercises. If there is tension or fatigue, focusing on the exercise becomes difficult. Tensions in the mind and the body draw the attention of the player, and fatigue weakens the power of focusing. If you have patience enough to do the circle of excellence training after a relaxation exercise like Shavasana, Yoga Nidra or Nyasa, it is very beneficial. You must remember to relax as much as possible in the beginning itself.

- Mentally, draw a large circle in front of you of the colour of your choice.

  Comments: In this step, colour and choice are two important concepts. As you progress in the skill of visualization, you are able to distinguish colours and shapes. The choice is very vital. If you get a feeling that something is thrust on you or you are being forced to do it, you develop adversarial feeling towards the action and the mood to excel is lost. Every time you do this training, make the choice of colour and try visualizing a circle of that colour.

- Place in that circle all the qualities or inner resources that you will require to excel in the situation for which you are training.

  Comments: Just think in advance and make a list of all the qualities you will require for your sport, like strength, stamina, agility, confidence, ability to focus or refocus, sustaining the focus and confidence till the end, and so on. Sit with the coach and analyse your game and style. Think about the additional qualities required and modify your list. This concept is a bit difficult to visualize or imagine. For, how are you going to place intangible qualities in the circle? You will have to imagine that these are powdery substances capable of vapourizing in the air. The next step will explain why I am suggesting this.

• Mentally, step ahead in the circle of excellence and visualize all the qualities coming up into your system and forming a part of your personality. Visualize your best well-wisher placing his/her hand on your head or shoulder in confirmation of your having all these qualities.

Comments: You should be able to convince yourself that you have developed these qualities well. Then they manifest themselves whenever required. Opinion of others, especially the well-wishers, matters a lot to us. Touch indicates acceptance. Your well-wishers have to reinforce your confidence of facing any challenge. If the person is elderly, he or she would place the hand on your head and if of your age group, placing his/her hand on the shoulder is a natural move. We had experimented with shooters doing this training standing in pairs so that there would be actual stepping ahead and anchoring or the touch by a well-wisher. Subsequently, one of the shooters expressed reservation that the other player was her rival. I immediately agreed with her. Since the effort is to build up your faith, any such doubt lurking in your mind can be dangerous. So we went back to visualization minus the actual touching or anchoring as it is known. But whenever the number of trainees is restricted to one or two, it is advisable for the coach or a parent to actually touch the player as this step comes up. Once this is done a few times, the player finds it easy to visualize the touch of the well-wisher, or the positive touch of a person giving the player blessings to win.

- Mentally, step back out of the circle of excellence. Visualize yourself in the situation for which you are training and identify the signals there, familiarizing with them. On the background of the situation select a particular signal, observing which you will get the confidence of all the qualities in the circle of excellence being available to you in abundance.

  Comments: There is no place for rejection or negativity in the circle of excellence. Since the process of selection of a particular signal involves rejecting the rest of them, you should come out of the circle and then select. Benefit of the feeling of choice is there in this step also. But you have to be careful in selecting the signals. It should be available to you to observe whenever you want to do so. If you lose focus during the match, refocusing can be done by observing the signal. In the billiards match I mentioned earlier, I had selected the umpire making the toss as my choice. So, I just observed the umpire as he made the toss and told myself that I was ready. Luckily for me, the flow lasted throughout the match. If I had lost the focus, I could not have asked the umpire to do the toss again. So my signal was not available to me. Choose any signal you like but it should be available for you to observe at any time during the match. I shifted my signal to the tip of my cue on the background of the table on which I would be playing the match. That signal has served me very well all along.

- Mentally, step ahead and stand in the circle of excellence. Visualize yourself in the situation again and calibrate the signal. See yourself observing the signal and performing at your best in perfect poise and focus.

  Comments: A relation has to be established between the signal chosen and your excellence. Make sure you visualize the beginning, some part of the middle and the end of the competition or the match. You should visualize all the parts of the skill, observation, choice of response and its execution. Visualize the result of your action also. See yourself taking note of all the signals at the venue like spectator behaviour, judgements by the referee, brilliance on the part of the opponent, and so on. Then visualize yourself remaining fully focused on the technique and performing with courage and confidence. Picture yourself observing your favourite signal off and on and feel the surge of confidence and deep focus.

- Visualize a good finish of the event. Feel the joy of excellence and picture the response of all others to your brilliance. See the natural consequences of your performance taking place.

Comments: You will have to maintain the same depth of focus a little longer than the time of completion of the event. This has to be practised in performance and visualization sessions also. Otherwise you tend to lose the grip towards the end of the event. Visualize the successful completion of the match or competition. If you are a tennis player, visualize yourself scoring the last point and then going and shaking hands with the opponent and the referee. It will give a clear message to the inner power that you want to win. The feeling of joy is always associated with your excellence. If you have practised reliving the best moments from the past and the feel joy, you will be able to do that in this exercise also. Then the response of others is a very vital factor and you must get into the habit of visualizing how others react to your excellence. Then the negativization caused by imaginary condemnation by others is checked. Seeing the consequences of your excellence gives a clear indication to your inner power about the direction of your efforts.

The circle of excellence is an excellent visualization method and if you practise it regularly, the benefits will be immense.

ACTION POINTS

- Sit comfortably, focus on your breathing and allow yourself to relax completely. Include the nerve centre at the top of your head in the focus and visualize that nerve centre sending messages of total relaxation all over your body. Feel the tensions and fatigue in your system disappearing.

- Mentally, draw a large circle in front of you of the colour of your choice.

- Place in that circle all the qualities or inner resources that you will require to excel in the situation for which you are training.

- Mentally, step ahead in the circle of excellence and visualize all the qualities coming up into your system and forming a part of your personality.

- Mentally, step back, out of the circle of excellence. Visualize yourself in the situation for which you are training and identify the signals there.

- Mentally, step ahead and stand inside the circle of excellence, visualizing yourself in the situation again and performing at your best.

- Visualize a good finish for the event and a positive response from your well-wishers.

18

Improving
Attention-Focus

PRANA DHARANA, SOHAM CHANT AND PRANAYAMA

As a continuous process, breathing is our permanent link with the present and also with life. Every incoming breath brings in fresh energy known in yoga as prana and each outgoing breath takes away the waste created by the burning and using up of the energy. We do not make full use of the ongoing energizing and purifying process of breathing. No care is taken to cleanse the lungs by emptying them fully. This is required for removing all the waste brought into them by the blood cells from all over the body. We also do not fill the lungs properly while breathing in, depriving ourselves of a lot of fresh energy. Though breathing is an involuntary process, it has a voluntary component also. Getting involved consciously with the process of breathing is known as Prana Dharana, or focus on breathing. Just focusing on breathing brings you in the present, which marks the beginning of concentration. Make this a habit and you are on the path of becoming a champion.

Bringing and then keeping the focus on breathing enables you to remain in the present. All challenges are to be faced in the present. So you automatically become better equipped to meet the challenges. But it is not easy to keep the focus on breathing as your *wani* and mind go on indulging in verbal and non-verbal thought processes and disrupt your concentration. *Wani* brings signals by means of words and the mind starts responding; or the mind gets involved with some experience from the past or future or from its imagination and your focus gets disrupted again. If you want to concentrate, the main task is to keep these two powers together. Here again, the prana can play a vital role. The chant of *so* with each incoming breath and *ham* with the outgoing breath, of course, mentally, works wonders in this regard. While chanting the mantra, breathing is included in the focus, making you stay in the present. The *wani* is busy with the chant and the mind has to be kept engaged with the meaning of the mantra.

The mantra means that I am the universal energy or power which enters my body with every breath. This power alone runs the whole universe and also my system. The chant done with focus on the meaning, builds up, along with each breath, not only the ability to concentrate, but also develops confidence. For once you identify yourself with that power, you have nothing to fear. *Wani* remains busy uttering the *so* and *ham* chants and the mind keeps itself involved with the meaning and both, together, are focused on breathing. So concentration is no more a problem. You can choose any object or event and shift the focus to it and you will find that the depth of concentration achieved by the chant also gets transferred to the thing chosen.

Another fact is that we do not make proper use of the breathing process. Lungs are not emptied fully and there is no attempt to fill them completely. As a result, we do not draw sufficient benefits from this energy-giving process. Breathing is meant to replace the waste in the body by fresh energy. If it is not done properly, the waste remains in the body and supply of fresh energy is also inadequate. This gives rise to a fatigue syndrome and also creates quite a few health problems.

Left to itself, your system draws the minimum of energy through breathing. The natural rhythm is, therefore, a bit shallow. Efforts to interfere with this rhythm involve a voluntary process, which is known as Pranayama in yoga. Bringing your focus on breathing and remaining aware of it is also a type of Pranayama. The next step is deep breathing. You should make it a point to empty your lungs completely while breathing out. If you draw in the stomach while breathing out, the diaphragm between the stomach and the chest is pushed up and more used air gets thrown out from the lungs. When you breathe in, let the stomach loose so that the diaphragm will be pushed down and the lungs will get filled to the capacity by the fresh air bringing in energy supply. This process is known as belly-breathing and it is also a type of Pranayama in itself.

Pranayama or voluntary interference with breathing rhythm includes stopping of the breathing process also. This is known as *Kumbhaka*. There are natural pauses after you breathe in and out. These pauses are lengthened in Pranayama involving Kumbhaka. If you want to learn these types of Pranayama, it is advisable to do it under personal supervision of an expert, as there is a risk of some health problems if these types of Pranayama are not done correctly. Interference up to deep belly-breathing can be done on your own, but Kumbhaka Pranayama, which requires the stopping of breathing, should not be done unless you have learnt it under expert advice and monitoring.

From my spiritual guru from the Nath Pantha, a religious sect in India, I learnt a very simple Pranayama which did not involve Kumbhaka. It is known as the Amrit Pranayama as it is supposed to give a long and healthy life. It consists of establishing a rhythm in deep belly-breathing without attempting to stop the breath. It is very easy to learn and quite safe, requiring no personal monitoring. In yoga, Pranayama is a very important exercise and has to be practised regularly. Unless you do that, you do not qualify for focusing on anything. In all sports, you require a very high quality of focus. Our experiments show that this Pranayama from the Nath sect serves the purpose of improving the focus admirably. It can be learnt at any age and involves no risk whatsoever, while the benefits are tremendous.

This Pranayama is meant for creation of energy reserves and it can be started at any time of the year, even during the competition season. It has to be done very regularly to draw real benefits. One of the saintly persons used to do 100 of these Pranayamas daily. He was of the opinion that if one did these Pranayamas regularly one need not do any other physical exercise. He himself lived for 101 years in good health. His argument may hold good for a saint, but a sportsman, who requires energy in huge amounts, should not depend on this Pranayama alone.

I shall describe here the method of practicing the Amrit Pranayama.

Sit cross-legged if you can. Otherwise you can sit on a chair. If you are not used to sitting on the ground use a good backrest against the wall. Sit facing east or north, as these two directions are supposed to be sacred. Then say the following *sankalpa*, which is a statement explaining what you are going to do and why.

'Now I am doing Pranayama. Each incoming breath will bring fresh universal energy into my system and it will remain stored in the cells of my body. Each outgoing breath will carry away and destroy the waste, ill health and bad thoughts from my system.' (Actually this is what the breathing process is supposed to do.)

Take 2–3 deep breaths emptying the lungs fully. With the lungs empty, start breathing in. For a count of 8, breathe in through the nose and let your stomach loose. Then for a count of 16, breathe out through your mouth drawing the stomach in.

The minimum number of these Pranayamas prescribed may be calculated by adding three to your age. If you are 25, you should do 28 Pranayamas. If you do more of these Pranayamas, it will be beneficial. 50 to 100 Pranayamas a day are recommended. It takes 10 to 20 minutes and should be done on an empty stomach. Morning hours are supposed to be the best time. But evenings, also, are fine if one has not eaten anything for more than three hours. For the rhythm we were taught to chant 'Hari Om' 8 times while breathing in and 16 times while breathing out. Any such short chant can serve the purpose, and instead of counting 1, 2, 3 mentally, it is easier to count the chant on the phalanges and tips of the fingers.

PRANA DHARANA, SOHAM CHANTS AND PRANAYAMA

- Prana Dharana: Getting involved consciously with the process of breathing is known as Prana Dharana, or focus on breathing. Just focusing on breathing brings you in the present, which marks the beginning of concentration. Make this a habit and you are on the path to becoming a champion.

- Soham Chants: The chant of *so* with each incoming breath and *ham* with the outgoing breath, of course mentally, works wonders. While chanting the mantra and breathing, focusing on the breath makes you stay in the present; the *wani* remains busy with the chant and the mind is engaged with the meaning of the mantra.

- Pranayama: Take 2–3 deep breaths emptying the lungs fully. With empty lungs, start breathing in. Breathe in through nose and let your stomach loose for a count of 8. Then, for a count of 16, breathe out through your mouth, drawing the stomach in.

TONGUE LOCK AND TRATAKA

In 1990, I had met a practising yogi in Ujjain, Madhya Pradesh. At that time I was intrigued with some advanced focus training in yoga. Some of the terms in *Patanjali Yoga Darshan* were not clear to me. I had a feeling that the focus developed using the techniques mentioned in the aphorisms I was studying would be useful to games like shooting. When I asked him about my difficulty, he was curious to know why I was interested in those things. When I told him that it was required for focus in sports, he smiled. He said that I was on the right track, but it would take me years to study and build up the focus. He added that I was trying to study in great depths for a very minor problem and added that by the time I attained proficiency in the type of focus mentioned in those aphorisms, I was sure to lose all interests in ordinary things like target shooting.

In place of the advanced techniques I was talking about, he offered to teach me a simple technique which would serve my purpose. What he told me was so simple that I found it difficult to believe him. Later on, when I experimented with the technique myself and passed it on to some of the top trainees, the results were simply astonishing. The yogi taught me the tongue-lock exercise which meant that you lock your tongue and stop all its movements. It should not touch any part of the inside of your mouth. This had to be done in the active phase of the skill while handling the main transition point. In target shooting, it is the trigger release. The results obtained surprised all of us. Those who were facing serious problems of focus benefited immensely and even won medals in international competitions. For games involving movement, we tried locking the tongue against the palate, either by reversing the tip and pressing the lower side against the palate or raising the central part of the tongue and touching the palate with it. It was useful but the most effective exercise was the one where the tongue was left hanging, as told by the yogi. Those playing games of quick movement find it difficult to practise this, so we taught them the version improvised by us.

How does this simple thing work? Your tongue is the means to speak. Whenever verbal thought processes are going on in your mind, it makes efforts to verbalize them. Just try to sing the national anthem mentally. You will find that the tongue is trying to make imperceptible movements for pronouncing the words. This is how it helps the process of verbalization of thoughts. If you kill the movement of the tongue, by putting it in a lock, the verbalization process weakens. Since you are dealing with a non-verbal skill while you are playing your game, the less you think in words, the better for you. Distraction from non-verbal thoughts is weakened by this apparently simple exercise. But you will find that it is not so simple, since you have to break a long-standing habit. Why not start the effort now and benefit from the improvement in concentration?

Trataka is an advanced exercise in yoga which involves gazing continuously at a selected object. You are expected to bring and keep your focus not only of your sight but also of all your thoughts on that object. You qualify to do Trataka only if you have been doing yogasanas and Pranayama regularly. If done properly, it gives immense power of concentration on an object and later on an event can be chosen to focus on. The well-known practice of crystal-gazing is also a kind of Trataka. For those interested in developing sporting skills, short duration exercises of Trataka are recommended. One to five minute sessions of Trataka are found to be adequate. The time-span of deep focus required for achieving excellence in sports is normally not very long as it has to be exercised only during the active phase of the game. Initially, you start with Bindu Trataka or Idol Trataka, then you can do Mirror Image Trataka, and finally Jyoti Trataka. Each of these exercises should be pursued for a period of six months. After doing all the three types of exercises, you should find out which type suits your system and then continue with that exercise regularly.

A word of caution is necessary here. Trataka is a kind of advanced meditation. Sometimes you get attracted to the joy of total focus which you get while doing this exercise. You may feel like going on and on, but you should remember you have selected this type of meditation only as an exercise. Beyond a certain extent, increasing the duration of this exercise may not yield the expected results in the improvement of your sporting skills and if it is to be done for longer periods, it should be done under expert supervision or it can be counter-productive. Then remaining fit physically is a precondition for doing Trataka, and it should be done only when you are feeling fresh. It should be done in a dimly-lit room preferably in the morning. If you want to do it in the evening, it is better to do it after relaxing in Shavasana for 5–10 minutes and at least a couple of hours before going to sleep. After the exercise, splash cold water on your eyes at least 4–5 times, especially when you have done Jyoti Trataka.

Bindu Trataka

The word bindu means a point and the actual meaning of this phrase is gazing at a point. In a very advanced version of this Trataka, gazing at a small dot is practised. But for beginners, it involves bringing the focus on a still object and gazing at it continuously. Take a white sheet of paper of double the foolscap size. In the centre of the paper, draw a circle of three-inch diameter and colour it black. Instead of this, you can also cut a circle of that size from a black paper and paste it in the centre of the white paper. Then paste the white paper on a cardboard of the same size. Fix this cardboard on the wall in such a manner that the black circle at the centre will be at the level of your eyes, if you sit on a chair facing it at a distance of three feet.

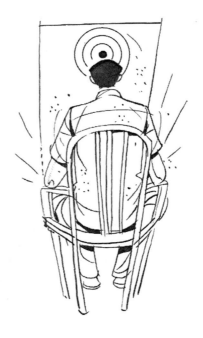

Bindu Trataka

For the exercise, you sit on the chair and gaze continuously at the black circle for 15 seconds without moving your eyelids. Then consciously close and open your eyes twenty times in the normal movement of winking. Repeat this four times. Slowly, increase the period of continuous gazing to 20, 25 and then to 30 seconds. There is no hurry to reach the 30-seconds time-span, and you may do it in two months' time. Then slowly increase the repetitions of the 30 seconds to 10 in another two months. Increasing the duration of time of gazing and the number of repetitions should be done only if you are quite comfortable with the earlier level. Remember to rest your eyes by the action of winking for 20 times in between repetitions.

As you gaze continuously at the black circle, it starts becoming hazy and blurred. It may also become bright and look as if rays of lights are emanating from it. Do not worry if none of these things happen. Your task is just to gaze at the black circle continuously. Lots of thoughts start clouding your mind when you sit for this exercise. You should try and detach yourself from all these thoughts and not encourage them. Then they will become weak and slowly disappear which, in turn, indicates that you are making good progress. Then you can reduce the size of the black circle to 2.5 inches and later on to 2 inches. The reduction of the size of the circle should be done at an interval of about two months. If the clouding of the mind by irrelevant thoughts persists, you can focus on the breathing and chant the Soham Mantra along with breathing. This exercise will give you tremendous power of concentration on any object and the ability to keep the focus on it continuously for the required duration.

Now, if you are worshipping a particular deity, you can use a three-inch tall idol of the deity or a photograph or a dark shaded drawing of the deity instead of the black circle. Trataka is done on this idol or picture and you may choose to chant a mantra connected to the worship of the deity while focusing on it. In this type of Trataka, you do not reduce the size of the idol or the picture.

Mirror Image Trataka

Mirror Image Trataka can be done after doing Bindu Trataka for six months. One may also try to start with it and continue doing it if one feels comfortable with it. Buy a good mirror of the size 8 × 6 inches and fix it on a wall in such a manner that you should be able to see the image of your face when you sit on a chair, facing it at a distance of three feet. For the exercise, you gaze at the image in the mirror for intervals of 15 seconds to start with and increase this period to one minute slowly over a period of two months. After every inter- val, relax your eyes for 20 winks and then gaze at the image again. Do this exercise for five repetitions. You may focus on the breathing and chant Soham along with breathing, but this is optional. Do not get involved with any thought that may occur to your mind, as far as possible.

As you go on gazing at the mirror image, it starts getting blurred and at times disappears completely. Do not worry, nothing is happening to your face. Actually it is a good sign. Sometimes the image may disappear and you may see only some brownish colour or some scene like a landscape or a sea shore. That means you are making good progress. But you need not sit for longer periods just to get this result, as you will draw the benefits of the power of concentration and feel confident, if you just keep doing the Trataka exercises regularly. This mirror used for Trataka should not be used for any other purpose and should be kept wrapped up in a piece of saffron cloth.

Jyoti Trataka

Jyoti Trataka is the most advanced version of Trataka as it involves gazing at the flame of a candle, which appears to us like an object, but in reality, is an event. The continuous burning of the fuel creates an impression that the flame is something constant, but every moment a new flame is being created. You start looking at the flame and observe the creation of light in the process of burning. Your focus is supposed to take in the whole process and not just the flame.

For this exercise, light a candle and place it on a table. Switch off all other lights. Sit at a distance of three feet from the candle and gaze at the flame of the candle focusing on the process of burning and the production of light for 15 seconds. Close your eyes a few seconds and try to visualize the flame. Repeat this exercise for four times. Slowly increase the time of gazing to 30 seconds in about a month or so. Then increase the repetitions to 10 in another couple of months. After the session is over, rest your eyes by winking 20 times, and then splash cold tap water on your eyes. During the time that you are gazing at the flame, think only about the flame and nothing else. If need be, you can chant the Soham Mantra focusing on your breathing.

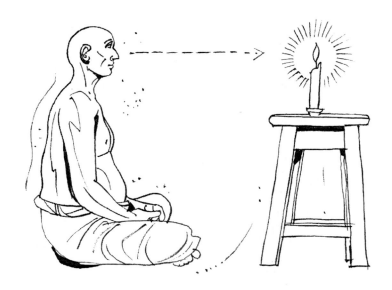

Jyoti Trataka

If you use spectacles, you should remove them during all Trataka exercises. When you do Trataka regularly, you should take two precautions. One is that you tend to become a perfectionist, which should be avoided at all costs. Then, you are likely to be temperamental, a tendency which should be curbed by controlling the responses to the behaviour of others. Really speaking, both these tendencies, if noticed in your behaviour, must be curbed, whether you are doing Trataka or not. Unless you are careful, you are likely to create problems in dealing with others. To boost up the team's focusing power, it is immensely beneficial to do Jyoti Trataka collectively, as it is one of the best exercises for the purpose. But care should be taken not to do it when the team is exhausted at the end of a match or a practice session. It is advisable to have a relaxation and visualization session before the Trataka exercise. At the end of the session, each of the teammates must remember to splash cold water on the eyes for a few times.

TONGUE LOCK AND TRATAKA

- Tongue Lock: Tongue lock means that you lock your tongue and stop all its movements. It should not touch any part of the inside of your mouth. This has to be done in the active phase of the skill while handling of the main transition point.

- Trataka: Trataka is an advanced exercise in yoga which involves continuous gazing at a selected object.

- Bindu Trataka: The word 'Bindu' means a point and the actual meaning of this phrase is gazing at a point.

- Mirror Image Trataka: For the exercise, you gaze at the image on the mirror for intervals of 15 seconds to start with and increase this period to one minute slowly over a period of two months.

- Jyoti Trataka: This is the most advanced version of Trataka as it involves continuous gazing at the flame of a candle, which appears to us like an object, but in reality, is an event.

19

Yogic Exercises for Relaxation

SHAVASANA AND NYASA

The skill of excelling in any sport is called *siddhi*, which is or a special power developed through constant practice. Your whole body is trained to respond in a particular manner. During the period of sleep and rest, the body builds up the cells required for expression of the relevant skill and the amount of energy used up in the activity is replenished. You will have to pay proper attention to relax, failing which, your body becomes stiff, loses its flexibility and becomes tired easily.

As mentioned earlier, a lot of energy is used up in resisting the force of gravity. If you are standing vertical and moving about, you spend the energy reserves at a faster pace than when you are sitting, and the rate of using energy is the lowest when you are lying down. That is the position in which you go to sleep and the energy-replenishing process takes place. If your mind is tense, you find it difficult to sleep. Sometimes, you may not have sufficient time to have adequate sleep and yet, wake up refreshed. The yogic posture of Shavasana is the best way to relax completely.

Shavasana

As the name indicates, it is an asana in the pose of a *shava*, which means a dead body. In this pose you lie on your back, arms slightly away from the body and the legs spread apart slightly. You may keep the head straight with the nose pointing to the roof or the sky if you are in the open, or turn it to either right or the left side, whichever is comfortable for you. After adapting the pose, surrender totally to the force of gravity and let all the body go limp. If you remain in this position for some time, you feel that tension and fatigue are removed from your system. But this may be only physical rest and your mind may go on with its activities and the *wani*, the power of communication, may bring a variety of thoughts and add to the mental activity. It is, therefore, necessary to calm down both these powers, the mind and the *wani*.

There is a very simple exercise which helps in calming both the mind and the *wani*. Just count your breaths. This brings your attention-focus, which is controlled by the mind, on the ongoing process of breathing. Counting is the task of *wani*. So when you focus on the breathing and count the breaths, both the mind and *wani* have something to do and they stop wandering on their own, and calm down automatically.

Simply counting 100 to 150 breaths, while lying down in Shavasana, is an excellent way to relax and remove the fatigue. The normal breathing rate is about 15 breaths per minute. So it will take you hardly 7 to 10 minutes to complete this asana and it is recommended for everyone. The quality of relaxation and rest improves if you train yourself to focus on various parts of the body and consciously relax the part on which you are concentrating. You can start from the head and go down to the toes of the feet or start from the feet and go up to your head, whichever way you may feel comfortable. There is also a method of inducing tension in the part of the body you are focusing on, and then consciously removing the tension, making the portion of the body go limp totally. You can experiment with all these methods and then select the one that suits you the best, for inclusion in your daily schedule.

In the Nath Pantha, there is an exercise known as Nyasa, which has been found to be wonderful for relaxation, and at the same time, it develops the ability to focus sharply. It is a very advanced exercise and I recommend you to take it up only if you are doing Pranayama regularly, or to start doing Pranayama at least before starting with this exercise. It requires a lot of patience and focus to do it correctly. The sportsmen, who made the efforts to perfect this technique, and practise it regularly have all benefited immensely. Once you become an adept in the technique of Nyasa, it can be done while sitting, walking, running, swimming, or while doing any activity. Practice of this exercise during travelling and the recovery phases of the sport you have chosen is strongly recommended. It helps you remain focused without much effort, reduces the tension level and preserves your energy reserves avoiding any wastage.

Nyasa means placing and in this technique you place a mantra on selected parts of your body. You focus on that part and chant the mantra four times with a *sankalpa* or thought projection that the mantra is charging that part of your body with its power. You can choose any mantra or thought of your choice for this chant. You should lie down in Shavasana, chant the mantra with focus on its meaning and include that part of the body in your focus. Initially, select the nerve centres at your navel, heart, mouth, forehead and the top of your head. All these are important yogic *chakras* and various benefits accrue by focusing on each of them. You may then practise chanting your mantra or repeat mentally the thoughts, or self-talk chosen by you for some time, focusing on one nerve centre and then shifting to the other centre.

The *sankalpa* for doing Nyasa is as follows:

I am doing Nyasa now. Each of the nerve centres I focus on will be charged by the power of the mantra, Soham, and by the prana power entering my system with every breath. That nerve centre and the parts of my system under its control will become healthy and full of prana energy.

Points of Focus Within the Body

Now we come to the main exercise of Nyasa, as it has been practised in the Nath Pantha. There are 27 nerve centres in your body. Focus on each of these centres in turn and chant one mantra four times. These centres are as follows: 1) right shin 2) right calf 3) right thigh 4) left shin 5) left calf 6) left thigh 7) lower abdomen 8) navel 9) heart 10) right lung 11) left lung 12) right shoulder 13) right upper arm 14) right forearm 15) right palm 16) left shoulder 17) left upper arm 18) left forearm 19) left palm 20) mouth 21) nose 22) right ear 23) left ear 24) right eye 25) left eye 26) centre of forehead and 27) top of the head. Six of these centres are located in the legs, three in each leg, five are in the trunk region, four each in the arms, and eight in the region of the head.

You may choose any mantra or thought of your liking, but you should remember that the attention has to remain focused in each for at least 20 seconds. The chant of *so* with each coming breath and *ham* with each outgoing breath is supposed to be the best for Nyasa. It improves the attention-focus, which is so vital for all sports. You will have to include in your attention-focus several different objects, events, sequences and thoughts while playing any game. The rules, opponents, time frame, challenges, signals, responses are all important factors which can affect your performance. The alert focus required for taking care of several things at the same time is developed by the regular practice of this kind of Nyasa, done with the chant of Soham Mantra along with breathing.

Record the *sankalpa* and the list of the nerve centres in Nyasa in your own voice or request your coach or a well-wisher to do it for you. Each nerve centre is located near the bone structure at the centre of the body part mentioned. As you listen to the commentary, focus on the nerve centre mentioned and also concentrate on the meaning of the mantra chosen by you. You will be rewarded with a confident and focused personality not only in sports but in all walks of life.

SHAVASANA AND NYASA

- Shavasana: As the name indicates, it is the asana or the pose of a *shava*, which means a dead body. In this pose you lie on your back, arms slightly away from the body and the legs spread apart slightly. You may keep the head straight with the nose pointing to the roof or the sky, if you are in the open, or turned to either right or the left side, whichever is comfortable for you. Simply counting 100 to 150 breaths, while lying down in Shavasana, is an excellent way to relax and remove the fatigue.

- Nyasa: Nyasa means placing and in this technique you place a mantra on the selected parts of your body. You focus on that part and chant the mantra four times with a *sankalpa* or thought projection that the mantra is charging the part of your body with its power.

PART III

APPLICATION OF THE TECHNIQUES FOR SPECIFIC GAMES

20

Cricket

In India, cricket is not just a sport. It has become a cult. No other sport enjoys such popularity and fan-following. It is but natural, for the game has a format which attracts the common man. Two fighters have to attack a citadel guarded by 11 alert warriors and any mistake can prove to be fatal. These persons are expected to steal runs from right under the nose of the enemy warriors. This format has given it a great spectator-value and they love to enjoy the vicarious pleasure of fighting a battle. Though it is essentially a team game, there is a lot of scope for individual excellence especially in the measurable skills of batting and bowling. Naturally, the art of fielding, which embodies the real team effort, gets neglected unless special attention is paid to its development.

The deity in this cult is the ball. It demands the full attention of everyone. The unique format of the game requires several role-shifts on the part of the player. The skills required for the various roles are so different from each other that there is hardly any similarity between them. The bowler becomes a fielder the moment he delivers the ball, the batsman becomes a partner in scoring runs by efficient running between the wickets, the fielder also has two distinct roles—first, of gathering the ball hit by the batsman and second, of throwing the ball on the stumps after selecting the side he should aim at. All these roles have only one thing in common, that is, the focus on the moving ball and they follow each other in a predetermined sequence.

Cricket matches involve spending hours together on the field. The attempt to remain focused for all this time uses up energy unproductively. The key to prevent this loss of energy is to focus deeply in the active phase of the game and defocus during the recovery phase. The type of focus required for the game of cricket is that of a bee. Imagine a bee flying in search of honey. It is very alert and quite elusive making it difficult to catch it even with a net. But when sucking honey from a flower, it is so deeply engrossed in the intricate process that it can be caught with bare hands. Nature has given it a sting to protect itself in such an eventuality. This is the type of focus required for a successful cricketer. And the best practice for developing such a focus is taking the role of a fielder very seriously.

The active phase in cricket starts with the bowler starting his run-up and ends with the ball going back to the wicket-keeper or to the bowler himself. Then there is a recovery phase which lasts till the bowler reaches the top of his run-up to bowl the next ball. Like the bee, all the players on the field must learn to go into deep concentration in the active phase. The recovery phase in between two balls or two overs is to be used to defocus, relax, replenish the energy by deep breathing or to plan shifts in strategy, if need be.

Cricket is basically a team game, with a lot of scope for individual excellence. The individual cannot win, it is the team that wins. The aim, therefore, is to cultivate individual excellence and blend it into the team performance. Whenever there is a clash between team goals and individual goals, priority should be given to the team goals so that the chances of winning improve. It is always better to be on the winning side, for the player gets more matches to play.

The strategy for the whole match should be planned very well, taking into consideration the capacities of the team members and the opposition, along with the condition of the pitch and the ground. It should be revised as per the requirements for every session and has to be implemented 'one ball at a time!' The players have to perform their roles as perfectly as possible in the time and space frame of every ball being played. Mental pressure is considerably reduced if the art of living in the moment is perfected. If the players learn to live fully focused on the present, the future is taken care of.

In playing every role, the major transition points which complete the role and involve a role-shift should be studied minutely. For the bowler, the most important transition point is the release of the ball, which has to be done correctly. Then there is a role-shift and he becomes a fielder. For the batsman, the moment of connecting the ball with the bat is the vital transition point to be tackled correctly and his role, then, shifts to that of running between the wickets, which is a partnership skill. As for the fielder, the moment of getting hold of the ball is the major transition point, when his role shifts to that of a thrower. All the roles require entirely different skills and the changes require a very sharp and alert focus.

All actions originate in the mind. It is essential that a cricketer learns and practises all the three skills, so that he can become a complete cricketer. Bowling is the only specialised skill. Every cricketer has to bat and has to field. He may become a specialised bowler or a specialised batsman, but at the same time, he has to become a specialised fielder. Then alone can he make proper contribution to the team's performance.

TRAINING FOR SPECIFIC SKILLS

Batting

The batsman is the hero of the drama that takes place on the cricket ground, and rightly so. The popularity of cricket has originated from the tough role that a batsman has to play. He has been tasked with attacking a strong fortress guarded by 11 skilled warriors with the assistance of one partner at a time. The aim is to capture the treasure of runs and, at the same time, protect the wicket. No mistake is allowed in this role as it results in the sudden death and the battle comes to an end as far as the batsman is concerned.

Scoring runs is what the game of cricket is about and it is essentially a partnership skill. It becomes all the more difficult as the partners keep changing throughout. A perfect adjustment with the partner is required as both have to complete the runs. Sixes and fours are like bonus earned occasionally and the plan has to lay stress on scoring more runs by running between the wickets, which is a different skill altogether as compared to batting. This skill must be perfected as getting run-out is one of the worst sins in cricket. All the 11 cricketers in a side have to play the role of a batsman and they must pay sufficient attention to develop the skill of batting and running between the wickets. It has to be borne in mind that every run scored adds to the pile of runs for the side.

Batting is the skill of connecting the moving ball correctly and beating the field-placing at that moment to score. Like all movement skills, it has to be executed by the whole body. Moving the centre of gravity for positioning is essential, as it maintains the balance and control of the movements. The batsman's time starts from the moment the bowler releases the ball from his grip and lasts till the ball is connected by the bat. The bowler, the type of ball bowled, the condition of the pitch, the behaviour of the ball after touching the ground, match strategy and the field placing at that moment are various factors that have to be taken into consideration while dealing with the ball.

Handle Transition Points with Grace

In a fraction of a second, the batsman has to judge the ball correctly, select the shot to be played, produce the correct action from muscle memory to connect the ball well, and obtain the desired result of protecting the wicket and beating the field-placing. The sequence of all these events and the rhythm has to be perfect.

During the delivery and the travel of the ball, eyes are kept riveted to the ball, but at the time of connecting, the ball is shielded from the eyes by the bat itself. The point of contact between the ball and bat is to be stored in memory only by the feel of the action and the impact. The area of the bat dealing with the ball also has to be controlled by the batsman and any miscuing can be disastrous.

Deep focus on the part of a batsman has to commence on the cue of the bowler starting his run-up. A couple of deep breaths with full attention, just before this point, will be extremely useful. The navel should also be included in the focus as it will ensure a better balance in the stance and subsequent movements. As the bowler starts his run-up, the focus shifts to his movements culminating into the point of delivery.

The bowler's action, if kept in sharp focus, will give a definite indication of the type of ball he is about to deliver. This inference gets confirmed by carefully observing the final movements of the fingers and the wrist at the time of release of the ball. Shot selection then takes place automatically. If need be, the mental utterance of cue words like, block, place, drive, cut, etc., can be useful in correct execution of the shot selected.

Beating the field-placing is the main theme of batting. Classic movements of executing a stroke or placing have to be improvised or modified according to the requirement. Effort should be to direct the ball after contact with the bat, to a particular point on the ground. Whenever this is achieved successfully, the whole experience should be remembered, verbalized in the diary of excellence and visualized as often as possible. Then the correct muscle response gets ingrained in the system.

The previous reputation of the bowler tends to affect the mindset of the batsman. This is full of risks, for a good ball bowled by an ordinary bowler may sometimes prove deadly, while a loose ball from a competent bowler may go unpunished. Strategy requires the batsman to be more aggressive or defensive, as need be. But aggression does not mean blindly slashing at the ball. A stroke requires a sharper focus than blocking as the bat is also moving, and connecting with the ball correctly is equally difficult. Reinforcing the correctly played shots, especially the transition point of connecting it by repeated visualization, is of vital importance. It helps to successfully build up the correct response, and ensures good contact with the ball. It has to be borne in mind that the batsman has to play the ball and not the bowler. Once the ball is delivered the bowler's role is over and he has no further control on its movements. By thinking about the bowler's reputation repeatedly, the batsman is likely to allow the bowler to occupy his mind, while it is the moving ball that requires all attention. In the recovery phase, convincing self-talk about the ability to face any type of ball and reminding one's self to focus on the ball will help building a proper mood.

Whenever the batsman gets a chance, he should study the style of opposition bowlers and behaviour of the ball after hitting the pitch. He will benefit a lot by visualizing a correct response to that type of bowling. The muscle memory of correct responses produced in the past while playing on similar pitch and facing similar type of bowling should be awakened by visualization and help should be taken of verbal utterances to strengthen the effect of visualization. This practice helps developing a sharp focus and also the confidence required to face the bowling.

While running between the wickets, both the partners should focus well and make use of cue words for communication. All the good actions of the partner beating the fielder by proper placings, his accurate shots and running between the wickets must be praised immediately, for it reinforces the confidence of the partner. It is also useful in establishing an excellent rapport between the partners.

In net practice, placing markers on the ground and trying to hit these markers by the ball is recommended to perfect the skill. Position of these markers should keep changing so that the batsman gets into the habit of improvising to hit the shots correctly. These shots, whenever played well, should be ingrained in the system by repeated visualization. Those who have a good timing should be taken as role models and their style should be studied carefully. Later on, visualizing the batsman performing, then repeating the visualization after replacing the role model mentally and getting the correct feel of the shot during visualization help in adding the shot to the batsman's repertoire.

Getting out to the same ball or a similar type of ball repeatedly can affect the psyche of the batsman. It can just be a wrong response being produced. In practice sessions and in other matches, he must have produced the correct response a number of times. The player should make it a point to remember and visualize these instances as often as possible. Then the risk of getting out to the same type of ball reduces considerably.

The transition point of connecting the ball correctly and directing it to the point chosen on the field is a link in the sequence of a number of events. The batsman is playing the role of an observer while watching the bowler run up and deliver the ball. At the moment of delivery and immediately afterwards, the element of selection of response is introduced and the body starts responding in the manner chosen. The transition point of connecting the ball, then, follows with the ball being middled and directed to the spot chosen on the field. In visualization sessions, the sequence of all these events from the bowler starting the run up right up to the ball landing on the chosen spot, both the roles of observer and a participant in the event have to be visualized as clearly as possible. This is where the verbalization process in the diary of excellence and the self-talk or cue word selected from it can be of great use. Reinforcing the correct response in memory should also be done at the earliest opportunity after playing the stroke. The coach can play a very significant part here by selecting the best strokes played during the day, for discussion and visualization, especially if the player is trying to improve in a specific area.

In actual play, the batsman has to keep on reminding himself that the main task is of building up a partnership, and individual score is only a byproduct of the effort. The teammate who is the partner at that time should never be looked upon as a rival for the individual score or the run rate. In order to connect with the ball, beating the fielder has to take the highest priority and the attempt should be to establish perfect coordination between the two partners for proper running between the wickets. It should be borne in mind that pacing of the innings can be done much better if the shot selection is correct. Then the risk of committing to a stroke without judging the ball or slashing at it blindly reduces considerably. Always remember to play the ball and not the bowler.

Bowling

The bowler spearheads the attack for his side and starts the game for every ball. Bowling is a closed skill, for the bowler has the choice of action and the manner in which to execute it. He is in a position to dictate the action of the batsman and this, in turn, decides the action of the fielders. Bowler's role can be compared to the soldier who leads the attack on the enemy territory and has to risk maximum exposure to danger. Courage to bowl to the plan chalked out and accuracy in execution of every delivery are the two qualities that a bowler has to develop. Controlling the speed, direction and movement of the ball in the air and after it touches the ground is really a tough challenge and this skill has to be ingrained into the system by constant practice.

The strategy for the type of ball to be bowled has to be decided in advance and all actions leading to the correct release of the ball have to be executed in perfect

Roles and Role-shifts

precision. The batsman's reputation, his form, treatment to the bowling till that moment and possibility of taking a hit from the batsman weigh heavily on the mind of the bowler. This affects his focus and courage adversely resulting in loss of control over body movements. A bowler really needs the courage and skill of a warrior leading the attack in a battle.

The main transition point in the skill of bowling is the moment when the ball is released from the grip for the delivery. Start of the run-up is another major transition point as the mental preparation and decision are transformed into the actual physical action at that moment. The strategy as to what type of ball has to be delivered should be finalized well before. Then every step taken for gathering speed and positioning the body for actual delivery is a transition point. The quality of ball being bowled depends on the sequence and rhythm of taking these transition points correctly. If pressure on the mind is not controlled, rhythm is the first casualty and the transition points are also taken clumsily. The bowler should bear it in mind that he is playing a single combat with the batsman for that particular ball and has to make an all-out effort to win the battle. A convincing self-talk and use of cue phrases help in maintaining the confidence and focus. There is a tendency to treat all actions in a routine and mechanical fashion and the mind is only applied while delivering the ball. If this is allowed to happen, the mind is free to wander about during the recovery and transition phases leading to the deterioration of the quality and accuracy of the delivery.

If the batsman has won a particular round by playing a ball in the manner he wants, a bowler is likely to feel annoyed and frustrated. The same thing may happen again when the batsman takes the opportunity of misfielding and scores a few more runs. The bowler's frustration is a natural response, but it must be curbed, otherwise there may be a drop in his performance level. Every ball to be bowled should be treated as a fresh round in the match. The recovery phase in between two balls should be used for making changes in the strategy, if necessary. Further, the bowler should make an effort to build up his courage and focus by self-talk or utterance of key words or phrases. He should use the final moments of the recovery phase for replenishing his energy by deep breathing. Then as he turns at the top of the run-up, he should shift his focus to the accuracy and rhythm of the actions, leading to the delivery and the actual delivery.

The transition point of the release of the ball from the grip is also a major role-shift point. Immediately after delivering the ball, the bowler becomes a fielder. The focus has to be extremely sharp for effecting a correct delivery and going into the role of a fielder. Whenever a ball has been bowled according to the plan, it is advisable for the bowler to reinforce the experience with repeated visualization of all the transition points. The rhythm and sequence should be remembered again and again and effort should be made to verbalize the experience. The actual delivery, the release of the ball and the trick played by the arm action, the wrist and the fingers, should be minutely felt in the visualization sessions. It is the feel of these actions that gives the bowler the confidence to repeat them again whenever so desired.

In the recovery phase, the bowler should visualize the type of ball that is to be bowled and its landing on the point selected on the pitch and the subsequent behaviour of the ball. In this visualization, he should focus more on the final transition point of releasing the ball. This should be done as often as possible. In actual delivery, full focus should be kept on the action and rhythm.

Fielding

Fielding is a vital aspect of the game which gets neglected because the efforts and results obtained are not measurable. The skill required is much more difficult than that of bowling or batting. In getting a hold of the ball, the hand has to close on the ball correctly. Then the throw has to be made from any point of the ground and within a split-second it has to be decided which side the ball should be directed to. In football, the goalie has to defend a limited goal area and can even deflect the ball with his body to save the goal. In cricket the fielder has a huge area to defend as a goal and has to gather the ball correctly every time. Mere stopping is not enough.

Achievements in fielding are seldom recognized and honoured, but good fielding makes the most significant contribution to a team's victory. As mentioned earlier, it is the best kind of exercise to build up the type of focus required in cricket. Controlling the thought processes and emotions and getting ready for the next ball can also be practised very well, while fielding.

Roles and Role-shifts

The fielder's time starts from the moment the bat makes contact with the ball and ends when the ball is gathered and thrown back to the wicketkeeper's or the bowler's end. In all movement skills, the player has to take care to ensure that the centre of gravity is moved. This is done to maintain proper balance of the body. But in fielding, the idea of balance is thrown to the winds while gathering the ball, whether directly or after a chase. Actually the players would do well to practise ground work in gymnastics to develop the agility and control over body movements and learn to break falls, like in judo. They also have to practise getting up quickly after a fall and throw the ball promptly in the right direction.

The best strategy for a fielder is to imagine that every ball is going to be hit in his direction and visualize himself catching or picking up the ball in various positions during the recovery phase. Every correct gathering of the ball and perfect throw should be reinforced into the system by regular visualization. Role models should be selected for the development of the skills in fielding and their actions should be visualized repeatedly. A strong mental effort should be made to replace the role model in visualization and get the feel of the latter's actions.

Wicketkeeping is a very arduous role in fielding. The keeper has to judge every ball being bowled throughout the innings. Besides the delivery by the bowler, he has to read correctly the intervention by the batsman and gather the ball every time it crosses the stumps. After a snick by the batsman, there is hardly any time to judge the direction of the ball and gather it, and for doing this, the keeper needs extremely sharp reflexes and focus. His task is all the more difficult if the ball is coming at him from the leg side, for the batsman blocks his vision on that side. Exercises of building concentration and attention-focus will be of great help to him, especially, Pranayama, Soham Mantra and Trataka. Reinforcing the correct movements by repeated visualization will also be useful.

A cricketer has to spend most of his time on the field, in the role of a fielder. He has to prepare himself to receive every ball being bowled, though only a small percentage of those come his way. Unless the challenges are identified and a total commitment is made to focus on the ball during the whole of the active phase, the player is likely to get bored. Boredom results in loss of focus and a number of costly mistakes are caused. Standing on the ground for a long time and occasional bursts of sprinting sap the energy very fast. The fielder should make intelligent use of the recovery phase and practise using self-talk and visualization for fighting boredom and maintaining a sharp focus. The attitude of the fielder also matters considerably. He should bear it in mind that he has the role of a warrior defending a treasure. There is the risk of negative or irrelevant thoughts clouding his mind and subduing his responses. He should zealously live the role of a warrior and contribute to the victory of his side.

The chances of success in bowling or batting increase considerably, if the player becomes a total cricketer. This is possible only when the art of fielding is perfected carefully. You get to play more matches if you are on the winning side. Without doubt, a good fielding side has the best chance to be the winning side.

LEADERSHIP AND TEAMWORK

In cricket the captain has to play a major role of leading his team to victory by making proper use of the talent available at his disposal. He has to judge the playing conditions and the opposition strategy and effectively counter it. While shouldering this heavy responsibility, he has to make individual contribution also to efforts put in by the team. The most difficult task for a captain is to maintain a high level of performance, for there are a large number of distracting factors weighing on his mind. He has to learn to shift into the role required by the game, immediately after the decision as a captain is taken and implemented.

This role-shift has to be complete. Then his performance in fielding and the specialist role as bowler or batsman can remain at the expected level.

The captain must learn to make maximum use of the recovery phase which occurs in between every two balls, two overs and two sessions. This time should be used for planning shifts in the strategy, changes in approach, pacing of innings or whatever verbal thought process that is required. Towards the end of the recovery phase, the focus should be brought fully on the breathing process and then shifted to the moving ball, which the bowler is setting in motion. Then he should live the role of batsman, runner between the wickets, bowler, fielder, etc., that the game requires of him at that moment.

The skill of captaincy requires lots of verbal thoughts like planning, calculation, etc., while the skill as a cricketer requires action and predominance of non-verbal thoughts. A captain requires both the skills and must learn to make the best use of the recovery phase for verbal thought processes. The breathing focus helps in changing over to the non-verbal action orientation, and focusing on the ball assists an easy flow of the skill.

The coach, manager, doctor, physio and everyone else connected with the squad should all be considered as members of the team and sincere efforts should be made to inculcate a sense of belonging not only amongst the players but also in the backup force. The task of telling the reserves that they are not playing in the first 11 is quite unpleasant, but their involvement should be ensured in the proceedings. The captain must insist that everyone gives his best in every role. Performance of the batsmen and bowlers can be judged very easily by the number of runs scored or wickets taken, but that of the fielders cannot be assessed so easily. The coach and the captain should take assistance of the reserve players to judge the performance of each player in vital skills like running between the wickets, stopping runs, taking catches, etc.

The captain has some say in selection of the team, but he can never have the team that he dreams of. It is his job to convert the team that has been given to him into a dream team. Whenever different persons come together, there are instinctive likes and dislikes. Then there is a tendency to form groups and try to promote one's own interests. Every member in the team has independent personality, some may be good mixers or some may be loners. As far as possible, the captain should have one-to-one relations with all the members of the team and must learn to respect the opinions of everyone. Regular team meetings should not be just a ritual. It should give an opportunity to everyone to speak out freely, the coach and the captain finalizing the strategy and decisions. The line of thinking should be clear to the players. Each of the players should get the satisfaction of participating in deciding the strategy, or at least being heard. Structuring of these regular meetings should be done very carefully. Surprise changes in strategy are required occasionally. But the captain should bear it in mind that the idea is to surprise the opponents, and not the teammates.

In the training schedules, playing other team games for diversion should be included. Basketball, volleyball, football are all very useful team games. Playing doubles in table tennis, where the partners have to receive the ball alternately is an excellent exercise in coordination. Actually, the game should be played by dividing the team in two sides and for every five points, one partner should change. Activities like going on outings and treks together provide useful diversions and help in building up the team feeling. Similarly, group games, group tasks, chorus singing, shouting of slogans, praying and visualizing together are also quite useful. Touch indicates acceptance. All the players huddling together to celebrate, high fives and hugs are excellent expressions to the sense of belonging.

Mostly, the team has a mixture of senior, experienced and new players. Every player has individual aspirations and goals and is interested in retaining his place in the team and getting selected for higher levels. If the players are not sure as to how they will be received by the group, their priority will be to protect their own interests. Some players become very aggressive and try to dominate others, and also influence decision-making. Some others tend to withdraw into a cocoon, and try to avoid being noticed. They will not make any effort to contribute to discussions, and prefer to wait and watch. Some players try to win over the support of others by forming internal groups. The captain and the coach have to judge these tendencies, and impress upon the players the importance of blending their excellence into team effort.

Informal and friendly behaviour amongst the teammates must be encouraged. But some of the players have the habit of making caustic remarks and talking negatively about the capacity of others. These can cause misunderstandings and sometimes result in unnecessary quarrels. All the players have to be very careful in their casual talk and the captain should ensure that the bond of belonging to the same team is made stronger by such informal relations.

On the field, the excellence of any teammate has to be acknowledged and celebrated. First name familiarity between players and informal verbal communication on the fields is good for team feeling. Mistakes, which are bound to occur, have to be pardoned immediately, and behaviour of the players should give a clear indication of this. A lapse in fielding or running between the wickets need this special treatment or the player tends to become distraught and is likely to make costlier mistakes. Moreover, adversarial feelings, if allowed to develop, will affect the concentration of others also. Unless pardoned immediately, mistakes can have a snowballing effect and can cause considerable damage to the team effort. It is essential to make the player understand and feel that he is not being condemned for that single mistake.

The captain should realize that his teammates are human beings and not performing robots. Each individual can have a number of personal problems, and not only the captain, but all the senior members should make it a point to know these and have a sympathetic attitude towards each player. Every opportunity should be taken to show that the team leadership cares for all the members. Common celebration of events like anniversaries, birthdays and also heartfelt condolences at times of grief go a long way to strengthen the bonds of team-feeling.

On home grounds the team has the advantage of the encouragement and backing of its supporters. On foreign grounds, this is missing and it should be made up by the team remaining together and shouting to support its members. The team leadership should see that every member of the team is involved totally in the proceedings till the last ball is bowled, for it has the responsibility of knitting the team closely together. A conglomeration of best players available is normally selected for a team. The real professional approach for every single player is to blend into a team for any match played together. Efficiency of the team leadership depends not only in identifying the individual's abilities and making use of them, but also in bonding them together. A well-knit team always has the best chances to WIN!

21

Games of Response

NET AND RACQUET GAMES (TENNIS, TABLE TENNIS, BADMINTON AND SQUASH)

The Challenges

In all these games, the skill of a player is expressed directly in response to the moves of the opponent and the object of focus is the moving ball or the shuttle. These are individual games but are also played in doubles format. One of the players sets the object in motion and the other responds, and then the responses alternate. These games involve accurate contact with the object while it is moving, and the important part of the skill lies in beating the opponent with the speed or direction of the ball or the shuttle, making it land in the opponent's area of the court or forcing the opponent to commit a mistake in returning it to your court. The match consists of points and each point is different from any other point, and no two points have any relation with each other. Your winning the previous point does not mean that you will win the point being played now, and your having lost the previous point does not mean that you will lose this point also. Even though you know fully well that no such connection exists, you tend to imagine one and lose focus. If you win a few points in a row, you must not think that you are walking away with the match and if you lose a few points in a row, you will be equally foolish in thinking that the match is lost. You must remember that these games are to be played one point at a time.

You must thank me, for I am making your task very easy. Your fans, your coach, your parents, friends all want you to win the tournament itself, leave alone the match. I want you to try and win the point that you are playing. Is it not easy? But you yourself make the task difficult by thinking of the whole match or the whole game simultaneously. If you try to keep the ultimate end in focus, you are thinking of the future, while the present is making a very heavy demand on your attention. The object of focus is either the ball or a shuttle, which is moving very fast. In a fraction of a second, you will have to judge the speed and direction correctly, select the response, position yourself to tackle the object correctly, execute the response selected by contacting the object with your racquet and direct it to a particular point in the opponent's side and get ready again to receive the opponent's return. I am amazed as to how you manage to do it, even if there are no other distractions like the result of the match.

Then there is the opponent. There is a tendency to try and fix the level of the opponent as compared to yours. You allow yourself to think that the opponent is better or worse than you, depending on the past record. If you allow an impression to prevail that the opponent is better than you, you hardly have any chance to win. If you write off the opponent as an ordinary player, who can be beaten easily, you might be in for a rude shock. It is not a secret that every player who is serious about his game (I hope you are!) is practising regularly in order to improve the standard. The level is bound to go high as you practise more and more. Now, you never know when the improvement will come about. If you do not know this about your own self, how will you know the level of the opponent in advance?

Even supposing you have some magic formula to learn about the level of the opponent as compared to yours, you cannot be sure about the outcome of the match. How can you afford to forget that age-old saying which is so true? *The better player does not win; the player who plays better WINS!* So why give up the fight just because you think that the opponent is a better player than you? And why remain complacent thinking that the opponent is easy to beat?

Actually, the whole charm in these games is that you never know who will win the point till it is played and is over. Even if you are playing the world champion, you may wrest at least a few points from him or her, and the point being played can be one of those. Just as thinking about winning the match or game during the active phase of the game is dangerous, even winning the point being played is a future event. You will know who has won that point only after it is over. So make the resolve to win the point just before the service and then shift the focus to the ball or the shuttle as the battle for that point starts. Then you have an excellent chance of playing better than the opponent.

Active and Recovery Phases

These games have a long active phase depending on the number of rallies made. Then there is a short recovery phase in between two points, and a longer one in between two games or sets. The active phase starts with the service and ends when the point is won by either side. The recovery phase starts with the point being won and ends with the service for the next point. Just like all object games, these games involve non-verbal skills. Any verbal thoughts coming in focus during the active phase are likely to disturb the concentration, which has to remain of high order to beat the opponent. I have heard many a parent remark that their child does not think properly while playing and that is why he/she does not perform up to his/her potential. Now my point is, the player is not expected to think at all while playing, especially during the active phase. Thinking, if at all needed, has to be done during the recovery phase. Even then you should think only about strategy and if any changes are needed, and that is all. Once the ball or shuttle is in play, you just focus on it and allow the response to come out naturally.

The recovery phase is to be used for rebuilding energy reserves by deep breathing and reinforcing confidence by strong, convincing self-talk. Remember to empty your lungs fully when you are doing deep breathing so that any tendency to gasp and take short shallow breaths may be curbed. Also remember to relax or make the suggestion of relaxing. Make full use of the energizing breathing process keeping full focus on it. Build your self-talk from your diary of excellence and make the commitment to fight all out for the point about to commence. The self-talk should bring your attention focus on the object and your technique and not on the end result of the match. I find that some players keep telling themselves something like, 'I must win!' but it is counterproductive. They will be better advised to pick up a self-talk bringing the attention-focus on the technique, movement or the object, which will keep them in the present while facing the challenge.

In the active phase, use only the cue words or mantras selected by you, that too, if needed. Otherwise, just focus on the shuttle or the ball and do what it tells you. Do not play the opponent. Play the ball or play the shuttle.

There is a mistaken notion that the correct strategy requires a lot of thinking. Actually, it is in-built in your system. You learn the skills of the game from your coach. By regularly practising it, your brain builds up the strategy required and the sharp focus on the object gets it naturally unfolded for you. Mostly two things happen towards the end of the match. The players get tired and the fatigue affects their decision-making. Then they get afraid of losing the match and go on the defensive. Their natural game is what they are best at. Fear of losing grips their minds and also the bodies making them weak. This is where deep breathing and a positive, convincing self-talk can work wonders. .

Transition Points for Focus and Visualization

In all these games, the opponent is a very important factor and is instrumental in returning the ball or the shuttle to you. Unless the opponent plays well, your best cannot come out, as the match will be one-sided. If you are in fine shape and can win the match easily, do so by all means. But never make the mistake of underestimating the opponent. You can become a champion, only if you can bring out your best, when your opponent is playing in the best of form. The closely won matches are more important for you than those won easily. That does not mean that you should be a late starter and lose points initially because every point is a match in itself and you should make serious efforts to win it. A point won at any level of the match is of value, as it adds to your score. In close matches, the difference between the two opponents is very little, but the bottom line is that the one, who surges ahead, wins. Supposing you play a tennis match and win it 7/6, 6/7, 7/6, 6/7, 7/6. It is a very close match indeed! But if you add up the number of games won, you will find that you have won only one game more than the opponent, the total score being 33/32. When you are aspiring to win, you do not have to be way ahead of the opponent. You must remember that every game, every point counts a lot in a match, at whatever stage they may be played.

Your time starts as the ball or the shuttle leaves the opponent's racquet and is over when it leaves your racquet. The opponent is relevant only when the object is making contact with the racquet as it gives you an indication about the direction and speed with which it will come towards you. As the object leaves the opponent's racquet, full focus must be shifted to it and the required response must be selected and executed. So there are two transition points which are most important for the skill to express itself. First is the contact of the object with the opponent's racquet and the second is its contact with your racquet. At the time of the first transition point, your role is that of on observer. You will have to see with sharp focus as to what is happening and judge the direction and speed of the object. Then your role as a participant starts. You select a response, move your body for executing the stroke selected and then actually play the shot. Though the ball or the shuttle has to be the object of focus, the contact with your racquet takes place when it is mostly hidden from your view. You need to imagine the correct feel of the contact in the stroke and observe the object again as it speeds away from you.

It is very important to describe the correct shots in your diary of excellence whenever they occur and visualize the proper response produced by you. When you visualize the shots later, you start with the transition point of your shot or the contact with the racquet and then gradually relive your correct handling of the chain of transition points that ultimately led you to your win of that particular point. These games require a lot of courage, as you are fighting a single combat with the opponent. Your verbal thoughts, in the recovery phase, should help you build up and maintain that courage. These thoughts can be guided very well from your self-talk based on the entries in your diary of excellence.

Do not depend on a favourable draw or poor show by the opponents to take you to the top. With that mindset, you can never become a champion. Plan and play the tournament one match at a time. Then play every match one point at a time.

Judo, Wrestling, Boxing, Karate and Fencing

With the exception of fencing, games like judo, wrestling, boxing and karate are played by using your body as the instrument. They require strength, stamina, agility and quickness of movements. The skills are required to be expressed in response to the moves by the opponent

Play the Moves, Not the Opponent

and there is body contact. The active phase lasts during the whole round, and the intervals in between those form the recovery phase. There are no specific transition points and the sessions of visualization should include the correct responses to the moves, whenever successfully played, whether in a practice session or a match. Watching the moves of the opponent, producing a quick response and pouncing on the opportunity to attack require a very sharp focus. Pranayama and Trataka are very good exercises to develop this type of concentration.

The chant of Soham along with breathing and focusing on the *nabhi chakra* are useful means to remain in the present. Deep breathing is also useful to remain focused and for replenishing the energy lost. In other response games like tennis, the opponent is separated from you by the net. But in these games, there is a direct contact with the opponent. You come under pressure by prejudging the opponent's level. If he is a renowned player, you feel diffident and lose courage just by thinking about playing a formidable opponent. Here also you should not play the opponent but play his moves. Since the opponent is in very close proximity, this is a very difficult proposition and you require a very sharp and alert focus.

Mental and physical warming up, planning the pre-match preparation properly, and remaining sharply focused throughout the match are the real challenges. Whenever you have been successful in handling these challenges in a match or a practice session, reinforce the experience into your system by verbalizing and visualizing it, as often as possible. Like all other movement skills, the ones required for these sports are also essentially non-verbal and the lesser you engage in verbal thoughts, the better. But you must find out a very convincing self-talk and mantras to be used as catch phrases to reinforce your confidence and courage. Relentless positivization is an essential factor in all these sports. Convince yourself you can win, and then you really can!

22

Individual Games

TARGET SHOOTING

The Challenges and the Transition Points

Precision shooting requires the shooter to keep his body totally still. His trigger finger alone should move in isolation. Some of the timed pistol events and the clay target shooting involve more body movement. But there is one thing common to all these matches—the opponents have nothing to do with the performance of the shooter. You use your own equipment and every shooter is given separate targets to shoot at. Your own scores decide your placing in the competition and the opponents have no interfering role. Still the competitors are under great pressure during shooting matches as they establish a link mentally with the performance of other shooters. You require a very strong mental control to not think of the opposition in shooting competitions.

Each match requires the shooters to fire a large number of shots to eliminate the possibility of a fluke win. In a competition, any bad shot can spoil the chances of winning. So the execution of each shot is like starting a 100-metre running race and finishing it. The game requires great patience, as it consists of repeating the same skill again and again. As a renowned coach put it, 'In shooting, you execute a perfect shot and repeat it 40 or 60 times depending on the number of shots required in the competition'. If it was so simple, all serious shooters could have returned perfect scores. But there are only a handful of shooters all over the world who have achieved this distinction, that too, only in two or three events. The world records in the rest of the events (there are as many as 17 in the Olympics and many more in other international competitions) are much below the perfect scores.

In precision shooting, the roles of observer and participant overlap, since the shooter can choose the moment of releasing the shot. The shooter has to fire the prescribed number of shots in the time fixed for the match. The tendency is to aim for perfection and attempt is normally made to release every shot when the sights are perfectly aligned with the target and the weapon is held completely still. But no human being can hold the weapon perfectly still. The movement can be minimized, but cannot be eliminated totally. Usually, the attempt is to do so and mistakes start occurring in handling the trigger, which is the action instrumental for firing the shot.

Holding the body still is a problem in itself, but a tougher challenge is to hold the mind still and calm. The goal which attracts you in the game is shooting high score. As you improve your standard in shooting, keeping score becomes very easy, for you have to calculate only the number of points dropped and these go on reducing with your becoming a better shooter. Shooting is also an essentially non-verbal skill. If you go on calculating the score, your verbal thought centre remains activated and the expression of the non-verbal skill becomes quite difficult. In addition to this, the fear of failure and focus on the mistakes being committed subdue your reflexes. Since you have time on your hand, you go on cancelling the execution of the shot a number of times. You are doing this in your match time. Naturally, if you overdo it, you start falling short of time towards the end of the match. This adds more pressure on you, as you become doubtful about finishing the match in time.

The mind is busy calculating scores, when it should be focused on the technique which will assist you to execute the release of the shot properly. Then after every shot, one's mind is eager to find out what has happened. Attention is drawn away from the technique and the sight alignment. The urge to look at the target is compulsive and disturbs the eye focus along with muscle tone even before the shot is released. All this happens when the body is required to be held as motionless as possible. Surprisingly, for a large number of precision shooters, this happens only during the matches though their practice session scores are very high, raising their expectations higher. Their scores are unbelievably low in matches.

Like yogasanas, precision shooting is an exercise for the mind as well as for the body. You are supposed to have mastered an Asana or a pose in yoga, only if the urge to move is quelled completely. The mind is so calm and focused that the urge does not arise at all. There is movement in precision shooting also, but that is restricted to the trigger finger, which has to move in total isolation. The shooter has to practise stoppage of all thoughts about movement till the release of the shot is over and for some time more, to avoid the risk of losing mental and the physical control attained for the earlier shot.

You should establish a rhythm of trigger release in practice sessions and follow it scrupulously in matches. This rhythm is the first casualty of match pressure. The recovery phase in between two shots should not be elongated unnecessarily. A positive self-talk and deep breathing with full focus towards the end of the recovery phase is strongly recommended. Then shift the focus on your technique and have the courage to execute the shot in minimum movement, rather than trying to stop completely still.

You will be shooting high scores very soon. Introduction of final matches of ten shots in all the Olympic events have added spectator-value to the sport of shooting. But it has become the cause of building additional pressure on the shooters. Bringing the focus on technique, remaining in the present and shooting the match *one shot at a time* is the key to handle this pressure successfully.

In timed firing matches and clay target shooting, you have to shoot in response to the target appearing or the bird being released. Here again, releasing the trigger in the correct rhythm is the key and any tentativeness in this regard will result in a poor shot or a miss. Since the time available is short, and no cancellation of a shot is possible, it is all the more important to control the verbal thoughts and focus totally on your technique. You may use catch phrases or words, if need be, just as you get ready for the active phase. The time in between two series or shots should be utilized in convincing self-talk, rather than allowing the mind to get focused on the points scored till then or the number of points required to win a medal. In timed fire pistol matches, focus on shooting one series at a time and live in that time span. In clay target shooting, live in the shot or the pair of shots that are required to be fired at a time.

Your capacity of hitting good shots is developed by constant practice. Whenever you have executed a brilliant shot, relive it in a visualization session at the earliest opportunity. This will help reinforce the muscle memory and produce consistent good results. Regular exercises of Pranayama and Nyasa are recommended. Daily visualization sessions and circle of excellence training have been found to be extremely useful to handle match pressure. Practice of Trataka and yogasanas regularly are also beneficial. The technique of tongue mentioned earlier, is extremely useful to achieve the deep focus required for this non-verbal skill.

Target shooting is a wonderful sport. It gives you the power of hitting a target accurately at a distance, and executing a good shot is a great joy. If you take up competitive shooting you must build up the ability of living fully in the present within the span of the shot being released. Then you will be winning matches also with high scores and records, which will bring additional joy.

Here are some tips for maintaining balance of mind. You may add to them or modify them in consultation with your coach and use them for your training and self-talk.

- Target shooting is essentially a non-verbal skill. Verbal thoughts can lead you away from the points of focus. In the active phase, no verbal thoughts are needed. Focus on the actual action, the technique and the sequence that you have to follow. Maintain a sharp attention-focus on the things you are doing.

- It is natural to think of the score as a goal, but it should not dominate your attention when you are actually releasing a shot. In precision shooting, focus on the release of one shot at a time; in timed fire, one series at a time and in clay target shooting on shooting the target or targets released by the machine at one time, depending on the event which you are shooting.

- In the recovery phase in between two shots, use your self-talk for *relentless positivization*. Use mantras or cue words just before starting the active phase and immerse yourself in the action.

- Negative thoughts, irrelevant thoughts and doubts about your own capacity weaken your will power and spoil your focus. In your prematch preparation and during the match, focus on the thoughts about the technique, and through convincing self-talk quell your doubts and reinforce the will power.

- Give up the habit of focusing on thoughts weakening your will power, whether you are on the range, or elsewhere. Do not talk about the negative experiences except during the analysis sessions with your coach. End up these sessions with positive thoughts, visualization, and resolve for following your schedules scrupulously.

- Never keep your focus on failures or mistakes by talking about them frequently. Learn from the failures and mistakes and drop them from your memory and the system. *Never try to justify them.*

- In target shooting, mental discipline is vital. After the release of the shot, there is a *follow through*, in which you continue doing the same action as in the release of the shot for some time more. Your mind has the urge to rush to see the result. This is very strong and can disturb the shot even before the release. Train your mind to follow through every shot or series you fire.

- Practise to maintain your focus throughout the match and for some time more. Strengthen your resolve to focus on the technique by self-talk in the last few shots of the match which finishes only with the last shot or the series getting over.

- Your bad shots will appear somewhere and the good shots will also appear somewhere. Do not get frightened when the bad shots appear together and do not get over excited for good shots appearing together. Your resolve should be to try and shoot every shot or every series to the best of your capacity.

- Score is the result. It is your action that gets you the scores, whether for the match or for individual shots. Cultivate the habit of focusing on the shot release and drop the habit of focusing on the score.

- Establish a good rhythm in practice and follow it in the match. Curb the tendency to get the match over quickly. It is an indication of excessive pressure. Your rhythm is the key to confident release of the shot.

- Deep belly breathing in between two shots or series with full focus on breath brings and keeps your attention focused in the present. Shift it to what you are doing and maintain it there till the follow through is over.

- I recommend Bindu Trataka or Mirror Trataka for precision shooters and Jyoti Trataka for the timed fire and clay target shooters. Of course, they should find out which of these suits their system, and practise it regularly.

- Pranayama and Nyasa are also strongly recommended as they build up the ability to concentrate and relax. Nyasa is a good exercise for the recovery phase. You may choose one or two centres and continue Nyasa on them for a few breaths. Your energy reserves become available and you remain fresh for a longer time.

- Enjoy shooting. Enjoy living fully in the present. Enjoy the high scores that are bound to follow.

CUE GAMES (BILLIARDS AND SNOOKER)

What started basically as a pastime in a parlour has now developed into fascinating games. They are almost as addictive as the game of golf. Though strictly individual skills are involved, these games differ from shooting and golf in that the players take turns at the table and each of them has to start his turn from the position left by the opponent. So, there is a chance to affect the game of the opponent, at least slightly. But once your turn starts, there is nothing that the opponent can do except wait for his turn to come. Of course, the situation is reversed when the opponent is at the table.

In billiards and snooker, the champions make the games appear so easy. Actually, there is no easy stroke in any of these games, unless it is a sitter. But these people make every shot more difficult by trying to get the precise position of the balls after the shot. For strugglers like us getting the 2/3 points for cannon, pot or in off is an achievement by itself. The accomplished players, on the other hand, bring the desired position again and again with great ease and get their shots quite easily in a row. I remember Wilson Jones, the great master of cue games commenting to me (while we were trying to endure the fiercely fought match between two very mediocre players), 'I really admire these players. They go from difficulty to difficulty and still manage to score some points!'

Nothing that you do in these games resembles any other natural action. Unless you are looking for some small objects in between stacks of books on a table or in some odd place, you will never adopt the stance of a billiards player. But the champions have the strength, stamina and patience to do it hundreds of times over and again, and build up huge breaks.

The cue games are difficult to master; the facilities to play are also not easily available; still they provide an excellent diversion to escape from the stress created in the other walks of life. But a word of caution is needed here. You must take the game a little seriously and try to focus on it, otherwise your mind will become free to fret over the past and worry about the future. In practice games, you do not have to become a champion, but you must be acceptable to the other players as a partner or opponent. Just the attempt to focus on what you are doing can work wonders for your game.

But competitive billiards or snooker are different propositions. You need to spend a lot of quality time in developing the basics and later on the niceties of cue delivery—the strength, sighting, aiming, stunning, screwing back, running and check side and so many other details of the skill required for the game. Then you start getting good breaks consistently and start entering competitions. The importance of the result of the match puts a lot of pressure, in addition to the feeling of having to perform before a crowd weighing heavily on your mind. Then the risk of handing over the advantage to the opponent by making mistakes tends to make you unsure about your ability to tackle even slightly difficult situations.

You become overcautious and defensive. Fear of failure and the excitement of playing in strange conditions affect your body–mind coordination and you find a tremor in your hand holding the cue. Luckily the hand forming the bridge is resting on the table, otherwise, it also would be trembling. Your feet also start feeling wobbly. There are butterflies in the stomach. All this has never happened in your practice sessions. Then how do you practise handling these conditions?

First and foremost, do not link these feelings with failure. They are giving you an indication that you are keen to perform well. It is a mixture of the feeling of curiousity and fear about the unknown future. Overcome the feeling of fear by a convincing self-talk and reinforce the feeling of curiosity. The second important suggestion is to play as many matches as possible. How will you learn to respond to a feeling which comes only in matches, unless you play them? You will find that the feeling comes whenever you play a match and disappears as you start focusing on what you are doing. There is no substitute for match experience. You will also realize that the tremor does not make much of a difference to your game, and as you gain experience, it starts disappearing earlier.

Analyse the game you have chosen with an experienced player or your coach. You have two major roles— one as a performer when you are at the table and the other is that of a spectator. When the opponent is playing, watch his game and try to focus on his excellence. Your self-talk must convince you that you will be able to play at your best when your turn comes. If you build up the courage to enjoy your opponent's excellence, it becomes a signal for your best to come out. Then the flow of your skill becomes ideal and you enter a special zone of focus which is reserved only for champions. Once you enter the role of the performer, you need not even remember who your opponent is, except in shot selection. You have to be careful in selecting your shots when you are playing Geet Sethi or Pankaj Advani. But once you form the bridge on the table to execute the shot selected, everything including the opponent should go totally out of focus.

Whenever you have done really well in a match, verbalize the experience in your diary of excellence, especially the poise and the depth of concentration you have achieved. Identify the thought processes which helped you to reach the natural skill flow. You will be able to develop a good self-talk to convince you of your excellence. Since it is coming out of your own experience, your system will accept it readily.

Your visit consists of a large number of shots. The period from your starting to address the cue ball for delivery of the stroke, till your completion of the cue action forms the active phase. Your movement around the table to position yourself for the next shot forms the recovery phase, and the most important transition point is the moment of the actual contact between the cue tip and the cue ball. You will have to plan the strategy and modification to it, if any, required during the recovery phase. Since you are likely to take quite some time for big breaks, it is advisable to use the recovery phase after a few shots for deep belly-breathing and consciously relaxing a part of your body. This is of great help in replenishing the energy and reinforcing confidence. Self-talk, if any, should be done in the recovery phase only. Once you are tackling the active phase, all verbal thoughts should stop as you are expressing a non-verbal skill. You may like to use some cue phrases occasionally, as you start focusing for the active phase.

When your opponent is at the table, it is a long recovery phase for you. As mentioned earlier, you may watch the opponent's game and focus on his excellence. Instead of this or along with this, you can do the exercise of Nyasa. If you do this, you will be able to attain the depth of concentration required, during your visit, quite easily. If you feel that the whole cycle of Nyasa will require too much of concentration, just focus on the *chakra* at the navel and chant Soham along with breathing. These exercises will help you remain fresh and save you from boredom.

Play as many tournaments as you can. I enjoyed several years of league tournaments in Mumbai in billiards and snooker in the seventies and eighties. It was a wonderful concept. There were handicaps given to lesser mortals like us, and since the matches were on league basis, we got to play all the games, whether we won or lost. I had the opportunity of playing a number of great players including the legendary Wilson Jones, O. B. Agarwal, Yasin Merchant and many other good players. It was a lot of fun, though some of the matches were fiercely competitive. After the matches, there would be an informal get-together amongst the teams. All the serious and upcoming players got the chance to play on different tables and against top players. It also developed a fraternity feeling. Such league matches should be started everywhere, not only in billiards and snooker, but also in every game possible. They will develop strength of character amongst the youth, by teaching them to take wins and losses in their stride and also to become friends and brothers with their rivals for glory. That, in itself, is a wonderful goal!

GOLF

Analyses, Challenges and Transition Points

Golf is a great and unique game. It offers one of the toughest challenges for a sportsman. In this game, if you play a shot from a particular position, you may not get the same position again for the rest of your life since the position and selection of the shot depend on a number of factors like the distance from the hole, condition of the spot the ball is resting upon, the direction in which the hole is situated, the wind, and so on. Then what do you practise for? The game has a very short active phase and a very long recovery phase, which is a unique feature in itself. Supposing you return a par score of 72 for the course, the actual time taken to execute these 72 strokes may be just about a minute and a half. The match lasts for three to four hours because of the long recovery phases involved. The actual execution of your stroke is the active phase and your locating and reaching the ball to position yourself for the next stroke is the recovery phase.

In golf also, you are competing with yourself and your opponent cannot have any direct effect on your game. For every shot, you are supposed to work out a strategy and execute it as perfectly as possible. The main problem crops up here. You try to be more perfect than it is humanly possible and spoil your own mood and performance. Bob Rotella, a leading sports psychologist, has written a wonderful book on this sport. He has very aptly titled the book *Golf Is Not a Game of Perfect*.

After a session with me, one of the golfers remarked, 'Why do ascetics go to the Himalayas to do penance? They should play golf!' It is true about target shooting also. These games bring out your real personality. I remember reading a parable about touchstone. It was like a mirror and reflected your true image, not only outward, but also the inner. Golf and shooting are games which demand total attention-focus like a deity to be worshipped by the devotees. If you take up golf and then take it too lightly, you are punished right and proper. No single round or match decides your level. It is your ability to reproduce the same form consistently that matters.

There is no recognition, unless you become a champion. The urge to tell others how you have excelled in some session is irrepressible. There is a joke about a rabbi who went for a round of golf on Sabbath Day. He was enjoying his game alone on the course. Enraged angels reported to God about this unpardonable sin. The God was also annoyed and said that he would mete out a severe punishment to the sinner. The curious angels watched the lone golfer and were amazed to see that he had a hole in one, the ultimate achievement every golfer dreams of, on the very next tee shot. They asked God why he was being rewarded handsomely instead of being punished. God replied, 'To whom will he boast about this achievement?'

The problem about this game is that the champions make all the strokes appear so easy that you fall into the trap of thinking that the skill itself is simple. There is no easy stroke in Golf, unless, of course, the ball is sitting on the edge of the hole. But that position indicates that you have spoiled the earlier shot! Each shot requires a superb control over your mind and body, a perfect coordination between them and the ability to execute your plan accurately. You may practise a lot and feel confident about every stroke that is required in the game. But when you are playing a match, you find that it is a totally different you that is attempting the shots. Your limbs appear as if you have borrowed them from someone for the game and cannot make out how to use them at all.

There is no limit to the expectations that a golfer has. You feel capable of handling any situation and even ordinary positions spring surprises at you. I have seen very talented and dedicated players, who have performed brilliantly in the past. It is very natural for them to set the standards very high. Imagine their suffering when they repeatedly fail to make the cut. Muscle memories of the past brilliance on the golf course can take you to the previous heights achieved and even beyond. If you fall in love with the accolades which have come to your share, and dream only about them, your muscle memories get clouded and performance levels drop very fast and so low, that everyone starts sympathizing with you. That is more painful than the performance itself.

For managing stress or facing adversities in other walks of life, golf has the best settings. No other game is played in such lovely surroundings. Spending time in such beautiful, scenic places is expected to calm your mind and make you feel the joy of peace. But the heaven outside cannot be enjoyed because of the hell within. You get so obsessed with the idea of playing a perfect round that you do not even notice the beauty nature is trying to unfold for you. Golf keeps reminding you that you are only as good as the round you have played just now. Your past excellence or the commitment to brilliance in future has no meaning. The present is the stark reality and it can be only as good as you are at that moment.

Handling the shift from a casual and unduly long recovery phase to a totally focused, controlled and very short active phase is the real challenge in golf. This is one game in which I would recommend all the exercises mentioned earlier for the development of concentration, confidence and the ability to relax. You should try them one by one and find out which ones suit your system the best. Pranayama, Trataka, Nyasa are some of the techniques which will help in strengthening your personality so that you can tackle the challenge of facing further tough situations at the golf course.

Here are a few tips for consistent, good performance in golf.

- Take your practice sessions very seriously. Try to focus fully on the action required for perfecting the shot you are practising. Read, think and discuss about it with your coach and other knowledgeable persons. Whenever you have tackled a difficult situation like the ball resting in the rough or the hollow carved out by a divot or a spike, describe your handling of the situation starting from the thought processes in your diary of excellence. Visualize these shots along with your other best shots.

- Golf is an addictive game. You, then, love spending more time on the golf course. Try and spend quality time there. When you are playing a stroke, whether in a tournament or in a practice session, get into the habit of living totally in that moment.

- Think a lot when you are selecting the iron or wood and finalizing the type of shot you are going to play. Then let go of all verbal thoughts and do what you have decided. Bob Rotella, a famous sports psychologist, advises golfers to be careful while selecting the club and the shot, and be aggressive while actually playing it.

- Practice in golf is not just physical. You have to perfect the skill of taking charge of all your thought processes and calming down your mind on command. The game is to be played from this stroke onwards. There is no use fretting over the mistakes committed, till then.

- Anger, frustration, sadness and annoyance are all negative emotions. They are natural reactions; you must learn to come out of these feelings by focusing on the matters at hand. Fretting over mistakes made in the past is the worst sin for a golfer on the golf course.

- These emotions are about the past incidents; they inculcate and strengthen the fear about the future. Fear is also a natural feeling. You should not allow it to cripple you. It has to be overcome. Curiosity about the unknown future should replace it. Use a convincing self-talk to control all these emotions.

- Treat the golf course as a sacred place. Relentless positivization should be attempted. Do not be afraid of negative thoughts; just shift the focus to positive thoughts. Use the beautiful surroundings to keep the focus on, in the long recovery phases.

- Keep your body and mind fit by proper exercises, diet and yogic practices.

- Watch your role models perform, focus on their techniques of handling themselves in the recovery phase and also during execution of strokes. Visualize yourself performing in the same manner, and try and emulate them in your practice sessions. Pick up every positive action that suits your system.

- Along with practice, develop full faith in your ability to execute a stroke by repeated visualization.

You must learn to believe in yourself, in order to achieve your potential.

- Try and perfect the technique of Nyasa. It will prove to be a great boon if practised during the recovery phase, as you are proceeding to where the ball is lying. It will help you in relaxing and remaining focused in the present. Relaxation resulting from Nyasa will reinforce your confidence and ensure the calmness of your inner faculties.

- Plan the sequence of your mental and physical actions for every stroke. Examine the lie of the ball; select the spot where you want to send it (keeping in mind your capability); visualize the ball on that spot, and then visualize your action which will take the ball there; do physical and mental rehearsal of the stroke; take the position and play the stroke with total abandon.

- As you approach the ball, shut off all the verbal thoughts and come fully in the present by totally focused deep breathing. Then plan your sequence and do the exercise of focused deep breathing again before addressing the ball and starting the back swing.

- At the end of the day write your diary of excellence and make a special mention of the strokes you have played well after a disastrous mistake. Take note of the thought processes which help you in bringing back the mood to perform well. This will help you immensely in developing the self-talk for recovering mental balance during important games.

- Plan your game for the whole course, and then for each hole, try to execute this plan as closely as possible. Adjustments will be required for a number of strokes. Make them and live in the time span of the stroke you are playing. Your score, the opponents, their scores, the end result are all irrelevant facts, when you are actually playing your stroke.

- Make a resolve right now to enjoy the challenges you are going to face at the golf course and to maintain your balance of mind at all costs. Why choose to go to heaven and then suffer hell?

GYMNASTICS, DIVING AND FIELD EVENTS

In the sports of gymnastics and diving, you use your own body as the instrument for the expression of your skill. Same is the case with the three jump events, i.e., the long jump, high jump and the triple jump. In the throws in field sports, e.g., discus, hammer and shot put, your skill and strength are tested in throwing an object as far as possible. All these are individual events and your performance has no relation with that of other competitors. You express your skills on your own.

But the opponents and their past reputation are well-known to you while you are watching their present performance. All these facts can distract your mind from the sharp focus required to handle the transition points in the expression of these skills. If the transition points are tackled correctly, chances of giving your best performance are very high. All these are very exacting events requiring strength, suppleness, agility and the correct technique. There is no question of chance wins in these events.

The programme or schedule in gymnastics, a specific dive or the actions in a jump or throw, require a very sharp attention-focus. The main skill lies in the perfect coordination between the body and the mind. This alone enables you to handle every transition point accurately with correct sequence. As a serious performer, you must sit with your coach, analyse the skill required for the action and identify the important transition points. Then, as you learn the technique, verbalize the experience of handling these transition points. Whenever you feel the joy of taking them correctly, write your diary of excellence. Then visualize these experiences at the earliest opportunity, and include them in your regular visualization sessions.

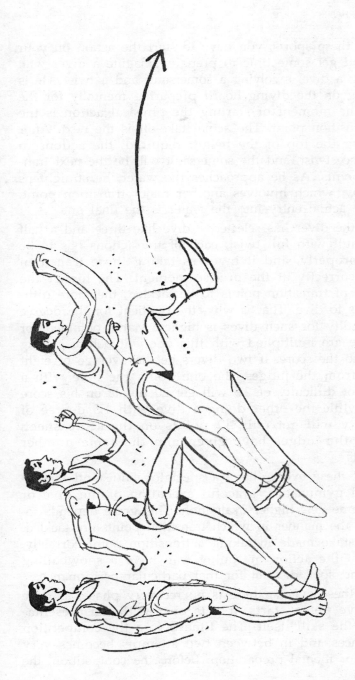

Transition Points for Long Jump

In these sports, you have to start the action on your own and get some time to prepare. Imagine a diver who is doing a dive, involving a somersault and a twist. He is standing on the diving board preparing mentally for the dive. The moment of starting the physical action is the first transition point. The actual take-off is the next. After attaining the top of the height required, the actions to commence twist, and the somersault will be the next transition points. As he approaches the water, he straightens his body, which involves another major transition point, and the actual entry into the water is the final one.

If the diver has selected a dive like three and a half somersault with full twist, each of the actions has to be timed properly, and it involves taking those transition points correctly at the precise moment. The higher the number of transition points to be tackled, the more difficult it is to dive. That is why, the quotient for the degree of difficulty for such dives is higher. Marks obtained for the dive are multiplied with this quotient before getting added to the score. If two divers get an average of eight points from the judges, the one doing the dive with a degree of difficulty of 2.5 will get 20 points on his score sheet, while the other doing a dive with 1.5 degree of difficulty will get only 12 points on the score sheet, though the judges have given him the same number of points.

All these events have a spectator-value and in diving and gymnastics, graceful execution of the dive or programme gets higher evaluation. This grace depends totally on the manner in which transition points are tackled. Any mistake made in taking a transition point correctly, either in the action or timing, can have a snowballing effect and spell disaster for that particular performance.

In these events, there is no recovery phase, as once the active phase starts, it gets over with the presentation of the skill itself. The time before the competition commences and in between two attempts becomes very crucial for mental preparation. Before the competition, the

Grace of Movements

schedule for mental and physical warm-up should be fixed in consultation with the coach, and should be followed very scrupulously.

For building up sharp attention-focus, the exercise of Nyasa is strongly recommended. It can also be done while waiting for your turn. It will reduce the anxiety to a manageable level; keep you fresh by preventing the loss of energy and ensuring its even flow. For the sharpness in the attention-focus, Jyoti Trataka is the best and should be practised regularly. Visualization of the past best and projecting it for the future event is an ideal exercise for perfecting these skills. In the mental warm-up, self-talk to reinforce confidence and poise, and visualization of the particular attempt is quite useful. Catch phrases and words can also be used effectively, just as you go into the active phase of actual execution of the skill.

23

Sports Involving Continuous Movements and Speed

RUNNING

Speed is a *siddhi* or a special power. It is a test of your strength, stamina and correct use of your energy reserves. You are performing at the same time as your competitors. Though they cannot interfere directly in the expression of your skill, their past record and the level of skill being expressed can weigh on your mind considerably.

There is a legend about one of the ancient kings. Every year, he would perform a *yajna* and give away all his wealth, completely emptying his treasury. Then he would go on conquests, collect fresh wealth and give it away in the next *yajna*, becoming a pauper again. If you have chosen any of these sports, you must emulate that great king. All the year round, you go on gathering energy and storing it in your system. At the time of the competition, you are supposed to use up all this energy, perform at your best and get exhausted totally in the process. Then, you start the efforts again to rebuild the energy reserves to get ready for the next competition.

In training, you will have to identify the muscle groups which are required to work for attaining and then maintaining the required speed for your event. Then, you should exercise them regularly, build up the required energy reserves in them by proper diet and rest. Once you have prepared well for the competition, you require the firm resolve to remain focused totally on what you are doing. Any weakening of this resolve diverts the attention-focus to negative thoughts and distractions.

Your inner power must be given this message that all the reserves should be used up in what you are doing. Your commitment to your performance and full focus on it give that message. Your resolve and focus make the inner power permit the using up of the total reserves, and occasionally you are allowed an overdraft also. But if the inner power feels that you are not focused on what you are doing, it does not want to use up the energies unnecessarily, and chokes up the flow.

Your mind, which is so eager for you to achieve the goals you have set, allows the focus to get disturbed. It starts entertaining thoughts about your opponents, doubts about your preparation or your abilities to perform. Then the resolve is broken. It becomes weak. Focus and resolve are the two guarantors for your inner power to use up the energy reserve. If they withdraw their support, the inner power refuses to make the energy reserves available. Right in the middle of the completion, you may, then, start thinking about the time and money spent on training and start regretting the lost opportunities for indulging in the pleasures of your senses. Instead, keep your resolve alive and maintain the focus on what you do, when you are participating in your event. You will find that all the energy reserves are made available to you and the flow of skill is natural and easy.

You should analyse the skill required properly in discussion with your coach. Running involves attaining speed by propelling your body forward. You have to place one foot on the ground firmly, propel the body forward and throw it ahead. Then the other foot is to be positioned on the ground for continuing the same activity. Muscle groups doing the work should be identified. Optimum utilization of energy is possible only if the working muscle groups alone are deliberately tensed up while doing the work and relaxed thereafter, when the body does not need to be propelled forward.

If the running legs have to be tense and relaxed alternately, other muscle groups need not be tense at all and should remain relaxed as much as possible. Of course, the upper body and the hands make some movements to facilitate the propulsion and maintain the balance. But these are minimal as compared to those of the legs. For maintaining balance, you have to move the centre of gravity forward, i.e., in the direction of your movement. Because of this factor, it is advisable to maintain focus on the *chakra* at the navel. This gives the additional advantage of being is close contact with the inner power, which is also keen to maintain your balance.

You will realize that landing one foot on the ground is a major transition point. The muscle groups pulling the body ahead are supposed to be working thereafter. As the other foot is crossing the one on the ground, there is the next transition point as the pulling action is over and the muscle groups which push and throw the body forward take over. Next foot landing on the ground is the third important transition point.

As it is important for you to defeat the opponents, it is also necessary for you to beat the clock. The proper rhythm and efficient handling of these transition points will give you the desired results. Once this starts happening, reinforce these experiences into your system by regular practice and repeated visualization, in which you keep the transition points and feel of the rhythm in sharp focus.

Breathing is one process which also deserves a major share of your attention-focus. This replenishes the energy used up and you should make full use of this facility. You should remember to empty the lungs when breathing out. while inhaling, take a deep breath. In short sprints, the energy is used up by rapid combustion and these races get over within a span of few breaths. From middle to long distance events, all possible attention should be given to the breathing process.

Energy reserves are stored all over your body. It is, therefore, necessary to develop the upper body also through regular exercise. Intake of proper food and good rest will build up the reserves. In practice sessions, focus on the muscle groups working and make the effort to relax the non-working muscles in between two transition points. For long-distance running, for every few paces, focus on one part of the body and observe the muscle groups work. Consciously, relax one of the non-working groups.

In competitions, you can fix the schedule for every few paces. For short distances, the energy has to be burnt up very fast. But in that short time also, try and focus your thoughts on the working muscles and the process of propulsion. If you do this in practice sessions, then you will be doing it automatically in the competition. Then your urge to think about the opponents and the clock, gets weakened and can be handled better. Like in all other sports, remaining fully in the present, focused on the propulsion of the body is the real tough challenge in running. You must work on it in your practice schedules, along with the other skills required for speed.

CYCLING

Cycling is done on hard ground just like running, but here, you have an instrument for speeding up. By pushing the pedals, the wheels in motion, which propel you along with the bike. Pushing the pedal down by your leg does the work of giving motion and speed to the wheels and the action of allowing the pedal to come up by pushing down the other pedal makes up the recovery phase which comes alternately for your legs. When the right leg is pushing, the left leg is recovering and when the left leg is pushing, the right leg recovers. This goes on for the whole distance of the race. Force is to be applied only when the leg is in the active phase and when it is in the recovery phase, it should relax totally. In practice sessions, this alternate push and relax phases should be perfected and the muscles doing the work of imparting rotation to the wheels should be identified. Rest of the body should relax completely. The positioning of the head and torso, to offer least resistance to the wind, require a lot of practice.

Cycling races cover long distances and require a great deal of strength and stamina. Deep belly-breathing and Nyasa are excellent exercises for replenishing the used up energy reserves and the focus required to send a message to the inner power of your resolve, to use up all the reserves at your credit. If you have perfected the technique of Nyasa, you can use it very effectively during the competitions.

SAILING

Sailing is one of the toughest challenges as an endurance sport. While working with the army team in Mumbai, I had a glimpse of what these athletes go through for several days to win their events. If you are working in pairs, there has to be a perfect coordination amongst the partners, and the strategies have to be worked out and executed, depending upon the conditions on that particular day.

But if you are operating alone, it is tougher, or that is what I felt. The race takes about an hour and a quarter and throughout this period, it is one prolonged active phase, with absolutely no respite in between. Stalling, balancing and guiding the boat are very stiff challenges and watching these athletes participating in a race reminded me of the fight put up by the old fisherman in Ernest Hemingway's *The Old Man and the Sea.*

In my discussions with the army team, I noticed that one of the participants was completely silent and did not take part in the discussions at all. I, then, asked him the reason for this and was informed that he did not understand English at all. Luckily he was staying near my house and we could have a few Hindi sessions together. I found that his commitment and the will power were of a very high order. With the discussions in Hindi, he could understand the arguments better and went on to win a gold medal in the Asian Sailing Championships in 2004.

Sailing—A Tough Challenge

For handling the challenges in sailing, you will have to undergo very hard training, and learn to take physical strain in your stride. Deep breathing and focus on the working muscles help in tapping the energy reserves. Make it a point to relax the non-working muscle groups every few minutes, so that the tensions in these muscles do not eat away into the reserves. Over and above all, love the challenges you are facing, and build up a convincing self-talk to reinforce your faith that you will be able to face the challenge. Keep a sharp attention-focus on your technique and what you are doing, so that negative thoughts do not gather any strength. You should concentrate not on the opponents but on their strategy, if need be, and make efforts to counter that strategy.

SWIMMING

Swimming is a different proposition altogether. You have to deal with an yielding medium and not the firm ground you use for running. For propulsion, your palms and the arms are used like pliable oars, since there can be a play in the elbow and the wrist joints. You need to take a grip on water with your palms, pull it towards your body till the pulling arm or arms come to the shoulder level, and then, push it. Finally, you recover the arms by drawing them above the water. In free style and back stroke, the arms do this action alternately, while in butterfly and breast stroke, both the arms function together. In breast stroke, the feet play a major role in propulsion and help in maintaining the body on the surface of water, so that it offers least resistance to propulsion.

The active phase of arm action is the key to speed. The arm has to move at an optimum rate without spilling the water in your grip. If you move the arms faster, they cut through the water and the body is not propelled with speed. If you move them slower, again the effect is lost and you are not propelled fast.

During the recovery phase the arms and, in breast stroke, the legs do not add to the effort of propelling the body. To propel the body again, the limbs need to be positioned so that the action of pulling and pushing water can start all over again. The muscle groups, working for propulsion, can relax in the recovery phase of the arms or legs.

But in breast stroke, the head is immersed in water, to maintain the body in a position to offer least resistance to propulsion. Air is gulped through mouth by raising the head slightly above water and then immersed again, and the breathing out starts. Because of this type of breathing process, it is easier for the swimmer to remain in the present for breathing is included in the attention-focus. But the problem is mostly caused by not breathing out fully. If you empty out the lungs completely, your muscles operating for the action of the lungs do the work of filling them very quickly and quite automatically. You need to practise this type of breathing while polishing your strokes, so that this can take place naturally in competitions.

In free style and butterfly, major transition points are your grip on water, as you immerse the hand or hands and start pulling. As the propelling arm comes under the shoulder, the next transition point occurs and the pushing muscles take over. Thereafter, you complete this push and take the arms out of water for recovery. During recovery, the limb should go limp like a rope and thrown forward to the point of immersing in water in a complete relaxed manner. Taking the arm out of water is the third major transition point. Back stroke also has similar transition points. You should learn to handle these transition points well in your practice sessions. You can use self-talk to keep the focus on what you are doing.

I remember a 12-year-old boy coming to me just a day prior to a long-distance race in sea. He was participating in the Dharamtar Mumbai race which was scheduled to start in the darkness of dawn, at 3 a.m. Every swimmer was scheduled to start after a gap of 15 minutes and complete the race on his own. The boy had been practising regularly, but was not confident of completing the race. Then there was the fear of swimming alone with only the lights in the boat with him to keep him company.

The race was to take several hours. The boy had doubts whether he would be able to finish and was quite tense. In practice sessions also, he had shown the tendency of quitting midway. His coach and the parents were quite skeptical about his ability to complete the race. I analysed his game for him and told him that just as he loved the water element and had chosen swimming as his sport, water also was deeply in love with him and would protect him. Then I explained the concept of the transition points and how to handle them. We decided that he should use the mantras, 'grip, pull, push and relax' for every phase starting with the specific transition point. He was to use these mantras for a few minutes, then think of the leg action for some time, think of the breathing process for a few strokes, think of keeping the trunk-region muscles relaxed for another few strokes and then revert to the chanting of the mantras with every major transition point.

This strategy worked for the little boy and he swam the race without thinking even once about quitting. He could keep a sharp focus on what he was doing and his system made all the energy reserves available. He surprised everyone by winning the silver medal and missing the gold by just 15 seconds!

You can also devise the mantras which work for you and maintain the focus. Your system will certainly get the proper messages and help you win.

GENERAL SUGGESTIONS

In all these sports of speed and continuous movement, the habit of focusing on the working muscle groups, the effect of the medium on the movement, and proper handling of transition points works wonders. It also takes care of the problem of your wandering thoughts. The focus on breathing and emptying of lungs help in tapping the energy reserves and also replenishing a small part of the energy lost.

The movement and strategy of the opponents should also be included in your attention-focus so that you may make the necessary modifications and adjustments to your own strategy. But once this is done, you should shift the focus to what you have to do to implement the strategy. For short distance events, the verbal thought processes should not be indulged into except for an occasional mental utterance of a keyword or mantra. In long-distance races, however, your self-talk can argue in your favour, stressing the positive points.

Pranayama, Nyasa and Jyoti Trataka are excellent exercises for all these events. Jyoti Trataka assists you to focus fully on what is happening, and then, you can pay attention to what you have to do for propelling yourself to achieve the desired speed.

There is no substitute for regular, sincere hard work to build up the strength, stamina and the skill of pro-pulsion required to excel in these sports. But during the competition season, you will have to travel a lot; adjust to strange conditions and may not get sufficient time to practise. Mental rehearsal of your skills, Pranayama and breathing exercises and doing Nyasa for relaxation and remaining focused, will help in keeping your skills fresh. Plan in advance as to how you are going to handle the sudden spare time on your hands. Use it for your fa-vourite diversions like music, having a chat with friends, reading, etc.

There is a word of caution about Jyoti Trataka. Do not do it for more than two sessions a day, and those too of not more than 10 repetitions of 20 seconds at a time. Pranayama, Nyasa and mental rehearsals can be done for any number of times you want and the time spent on them will be beneficial. If you are not in a position to do anything else, chant Soham, along with the breath and include your navel in the attention-focus.

In short, spend the spare time in the competition season in positive mental activity, rather than allowing your mind to get restless and bored. Guard against the tendency to fret and entertain negative thoughts. They tend to weaken your resolve and result in shutting off the energy reserves. Your self-talk should see you through these problems.

24

Chess

Chess is a different game altogether. It is essentially a verbal skill, while the other sports involve non-verbal skills. The 64 squares and 32 pieces in the game can present innumerable positions and the skill involves a lot of calculations. Every move has the potential of changing the whole strategy. After every move, the game comes to a standstill, and it remains like that till the next move is made by the opponent.

The active phase starts with your opponent making the move and ends when your move is over. The recovery phase starts with you making the move and ends with the opponent's move. Since this is a mental game, the transition points are also mental. The opponent's move is one major transition point. You start the planning and calculations of your move and come to a decision. That is another transition point. Your actual move of the piece is the third transition point which ends your time and the active phase. Taking quicker decisions and ending the active phase faster are advantageous, as limited time is given for the total number of moves. If you use up more time in deciding your moves, you may fall short of time towards the end of the game.

Chess resembles real-life situations. You have to live from the present moment onwards. Similarly, in chess you live from the present move onwards. Nothing can be done to the moves which have gone into the past. The moves of the future depend on interference by the opponent. As such you do not know what course they will take. In such a fluctuating situation, you will have to plan a strategy for the match and plan several moves ahead. Then, you should remain focused and ready to make quick changes in your plans and moves, as and when required.

A thorough knowledge of various openings, strategies and end games certainly proves useful for winning in chess. Deductive logic and correct use of all this knowledge is essential for proficiency in this game but decision-making is normally done by intuition.

Anupama and Raghunandan Gokhale, together, make a great chess couple. Both have been accomplished chess players and now they are doing a great service to the game by taking up coaching. Bhagyashri and Pravin Thipsay form another such couple I have come across. There may be some more, but I had the chance to know these two couples personally and work with them a bit, and that is why I hold them in very high regard.

Anupama came forth with a problem. She had become a housewife with a growing-up son and could get very little time for practice. She was finding it very difficult to adjust to the match schedules, leave alone to study and practise the new openings and the strategies and techniques available on the computer. Whenever she entered a tournament, she felt that her preparation was inadequate and was not able to even qualify for the national 'A' tournament. Her dream of winning international events again was apparently becoming an impossible goal.

I had an argument with her. My point was that the 64 squares and the 32 men on the chessboard offered such innumerable positions and moves that it was difficult for a computer also to keep a track of all of them. That is why some of the great players managed to beat the computer, once in a while. I told her that when she plays a match, the decision that strikes her as being the most appropriate is the factor really vital to raise her level. For taking these decisions, she must have the courage to stop worrying about the result, and implement them.

Luckily, Anupama agreed to experiment with this theme of allowing the intuition to have more say in the game. In the next season itself, she won a silver medal in the 2005 Asian Championships.

Children have a natural tendency and courage to use this intuitive judgement. They show the guts to base their game on what strikes them at that particular moment. That is why, we see so many child prodigies around, in this game.

Krittika Nadig was just 13, when her coach Raghunandan Gokhale brought her to me. She had been selected to play for India in the Asian Championship being held in Iran. She had become nervous and tense with the idea of playing accomplished opponents and the fear of doing badly had gripped her. These negative thoughts had tormented her so much that she was finding it difficult to win even a practice game. Finally she told her mother and coach that she was giving up chess altogether and refused to practise.

I was very skeptical, for there was hardly any time for her to prepare. But I found the child very intelligent and she could grasp very quickly what I was driving at. From the verge of quitting, she focused back in the game and won a bronze medal in the Asian Championships in 2002. It was a pleasure to work with this young talent. She went on to win the national title in the under-16 age group in the same year.

In chess, most of the players have this tendency to get bogged down by the eminence of the opponent. The fear of losing is allowed to take possession of your thought processes, right through the match. You must learn to bring the focus on the position and moves on the chess board. Actually, it is an advantage that you are allowed some time to reflect on the strategy and then, make your own move. But the fear of losing takes such a grip over your mind that you become unable to focus on anything. Naturally, you make mistakes in reading your opponent's strategy and your responses become disastrous.

The solution to this crisis is quite simple. Do not play the opponent. Shift the focus to his or her moves and play them, not the opponent. It is an established principle in yoga that focus on the behaviour of a person gives a clue to what is going on in his mind. Once the opponent has made the move, you have the time to study and find out why he is doing it. If you allow yourself to get frightened by his past, you have lost your focus. His past just does not matter. The moves, that he is making only now, should be allowed to have a claim on your attention-focus. The position on the board after every move should be kept in sharp focus. It will unfold your strategy for you.

The game of chess presents a very peculiar situation. You do not know when the recovery phase will end and your active phase will start. For this moment is decided by the opponent making his move. You have absolutely no control over it and just have to wait for it to happen. In this state of anxiety, you tend to become restless in anticipation of what the opponent will do and when. Then the alertness to start thinking about the countermove is lost and you lose valuable moments to bring yourself back in the sharp focus that the game demands. You will have to learn to keep your mind calm during the abruptly-ending recovery phase, and finalize your move as quickly as possible.

The chant of Soham with breathing, including focus on *nabhi chakra* is the best way to keep you engaged in a positive activity. It keeps you fully in the present and you are ready to act the moment you get a chance. Actually, the Soham chant should become a habit and should stop only if you need to rethink about the strategy or of making your move in the active phase. Once you make it, you can revert to the chant. Occasional reminder to your mind by the chant of 'focus on the move' or any other such mantra, which works for your system, may be required.

This is just a suggestion as to how you could tackle the challenge of handling the uncertain recovery time. A few deep breaths during the recovery phase with stress on emptying the lungs fully are also useful to replenish your energy reserves. The match can last for quite some time, and you need to use your energies as economically as possible and keep replenishing the reserves. Nyasa or conscious relaxation of a part of your body and a convincing self-talk to reinforce your confidence will also prove to be quite useful. In short, find out the best method of handling the recovery phase, so that you are in a proper mood and focus to handle the active phase. You may use any combination of the methods suggested above or find out your own system of keeping your mind active in positive thoughts, for this is the phase in which negativization takes place, and it is the most dangerous thing to happen.

Past games and moves, especially if you have made mistakes, tend to occupy your mind in the recovery phase. It is very dangerous to allow your focus to be diverted to them. Shut off the past by focusing on breathing, and then shift the focus to what is happening on the board. Learn to live in the time frame of every move. The chances of your winning will improve considerably. Relentless positivization is recommended in this game. That has to be perfected by constant practice along with the other skills required.

You will have to spend a lot of time indoors while playing chess. Your training schedules should include brisk walking or jogging in the open air, hill climbing, swimming or some other physical activity that will improve your physical fitness. Regular practice of Surya Namaskar, yogasanas and Pranayama will also be very beneficial for you, if you are a serious chess player.

We have found that Bindu Trataka is extremely useful for building the concentration required for chess. Ability to read the thoughts of others is mentioned as one of the *siddhis* or special powers you get by this particular Trataka. If you can read your opponents' mind correctly, what more do you want to win?

25

Team Games

FOOTBALL, HOCKEY, BASKETBALL, WATER POLO, VOLLEYBALL, KABADDI AND KHO-KHO

We shall progress and enjoy the fruit together,
United we shall be in excellence and valour,
Our knowledge and skill will remain fresh, my brother,
If we resolve never to envy, nor to hate each other.

This is a free translation of a prayer from the *Yajurveda*. It is used as the shanti mantra for the famous *Katha Upanishad*. All team games require a perfect blending of the thought processes, talents and actions of several human beings simultaneously. The training has to start with collective thinking. The strategies have to be worked out, roles of each of the team members defined, and then the skills have to be practised together. The training and practice sessions are very important not only for building up their individual skills, but also to mould the thought processes together. The attitudes of the players towards each other in various situations are very important for their performance as a team. The thoughts expressed in the prayer above are very relevant for building up the sense of belonging.

Think and Act Together

Only the number of members required in the game actually participates in the match, but there are several others outside the field who also have roles to play for the side to emerge victorious. All these have to be included in the planning and execution of the strategies. All the participants should learn to think together, dream together and act together. The players have to train themselves to remain fully focused and to live in every moment. They have to keep several things simultaneously in the attention-focus, in a constantly changing scenario. In football and hockey, 11 players from each side, 22 in all, are constantly moving and changing their positions, the ball being the centre of focus and activity. Every player has to be aware of the positions of all the teammates and of the opposition at every moment. His decisions have to be in the interest of the team and they have to be executed in precise and correct manner. The responses to the moves of the opponents have to be different from those to the moves of the teammates. Similar is the case with other games also.

There has to be a perfect coordination in the body and mind of every player, and also in the decisions and actions of all players in the team. The human body is in itself an excellent example of teamwork. The four inner faculties, mind, intellect, ego and the consciousness, the five senses, the limbs of the body, the bones, joints, muscles, blood vessels, lungs, heart and all other organs in the body have been assigned specific roles. In performing every task, they all work in perfect unison. There coordination is an ideal role model for the training of any team for their game.

There are six 'R's which have to be kept in sharp focus by every team member in his thoughts and actions. They are:

- **Rules.** Every game has to be played according to the set of prescribed rules. Your knowledge of these has to be thorough because ignorance cannot be the justification for not following them. Rules govern every movement of the game and breaking of any of them can be detrimental to the achievement of the team. The governing bodies of the sports organizations keep experimenting with and changing the rules every now and then. Not only the referee, but also each of the players must know all the rules in vogue at the time of the match being played. You must make it a point to study and understand each of them carefully.

- **Roles.** The team management must make efforts to define the role for everyone as clearly as possible.

Sometimes these roles may overlap. In that case, the players should be clear as to what is to be done. As a player you will have to learn and live the role for every moment of the game. This habit has to be built up by every player because the thought processes in that role should take place naturally. Then the decisions have to be in the interest of the team. Whether the role is to your liking or not, you must accept the challenge to live it fully. If you allow resenting thoughts to occupy your mind, adversarial attitude develops. Then the mood and focus are spoilt. Your observation and perception of the continuously changing situation are affected resulting into poor coordination and actions. You, then, become a liability for the team. Then there is no point in complaining if you get dropped by the selectors.

In regular briefing meetings, there should be discussions about the definition of the roles, analyses of the manner in which they are to be played and recognition of the excellence displayed along with tips for improvement. Live your role and help your teammates in living theirs.

- **Rivalry.** The feeling of rivalry is common to all human beings. If the rivalry is for excellence, it can be helpful in achieving the common goal. But when the rivalry shifts to recognition and reward, it spoils the team feeling and unity. You must be constantly on guard and should not allow negative emotions like jealousy and envy to creep in. Make the effort to feel joy in the merit and excellence expressed by anyone from your team. If you can make this a habit and the response starts coming naturally, you will be contributing a lot to the team effort. Your chances to excel will come, and you will, then, be alert and focused to pounce on them.

- **Restraint.** There are several factors contributing to your top form and achievements. Sometimes, they may not be favourable and mistakes are likely to occur. Do not fret over your mistakes and lose temper over the mistakes of others. You must learn to forgive yourself and your teammates for the shortcomings. Learn to look at things from the point of view of others. Once you inculcate their habit, you will find that it is easier to forgive. Every moment is precious in a match and unless you learn to forgive, you get stuck in that past moment. Then, it is difficult for you to remain alert for the challenges that you have to face in the moments to follow.

Verbal expression indicating that the mistake is best forgotten, and touch are excellent methods, to make your colleague feel being supported. The support from the teammates has to be there in both right and wrong. Make sure of this, otherwise the enemy will overpower you and the battle will be lost. You must exercise restraint in order that your team may perform better.

• **Response.** For excelling in team games you have to condition your responses. First and foremost, you must learn to respond rather than to react. The situation that keeps unfolding before you, the strategy of your opponents and the actual movements of the ball—all require not a reaction but a well-conditioned response. This should be ingrained to become a habit and should become natural. If the desired response is not coming easily, you must use self-talk to convince yourself. Your thought processes precede your response. Self-talk should remind you what line of thoughts are useful for the team effort. Make it a habit to induce these thoughts verbally and let your actions be guided by them. Once you practise it well, the process becomes very natural and quick. Then you can deal with the fast-changing situations very effectively. Your wrong responses can put the team